THE
MARQUETRY COURSE

To Uncle Tommy (late Tommy Limmer)

and

to Dad, my mentor and a good friend (late Stanley Apps),
we dedicate this book

THE MARQUETRY COURSE

JACK METCALFE & JOHN APPS

B T BATSFORD

First published 2003

ISBN 0 7134 8850 6

A CIP catalogue record for this book is available from the British Library.

Printed in Singapore
for the publishers
B T Batsford
64 Brewery Road
London N7 9NT
England

www.batsford.com

A member of **Chrysalis** Books plc

Distributed in the United States and Canada by Sterling Publishing Co., 387 Park Avenue South, New York, NY 10016, USA

ACKNOWLEDGEMENTS

What started out as a small idea involving two keen woodworkers, developed into a major undertaking affecting a host of skilful and dedicated people and organisations. Without their support, professional advice, technical input and most of all—their presence, this book would not have emerged.

We would like to thank the City & Guild of London Institute for providing the need for this book, members of the Leeds Marquetry Group, students and staff of the York College and the Leeds College of Art & Design; Stephen Hall for producing the professional furniture plans/drawings and 3D-CAD illustrations; Jeffrey Glyn (English master) whose 'red pen' kept our writings legible; Lorraine Trickett for the hours of typing; Ron Hudson—photography technician for the pictures in Chapter 5; James Lomax—Curator to The Chippendale Society and Temple Newsam House; David Stockdale–Registrar and Collections Manager at the The Harewood House Trust; Adam Bowett—wood and furniture historian; ALPI Reconstructed real-wood veneers; Ian Frazer—Conservator, and Kitty Ross—Curator for the Leeds Museums and Galleries; Brian Day for allowing his late grandfather's work to be shown; Giuseppe Rocco (Sorrento) for his 'intarsia' work, which is a constant inspiration; Gordon Wight (furniture maker) for permission to use his fire screen design; David Hawkins, furniture restorer; plus the following students and hobbyists who kindly allowed us to photograph their furniture: Tony Thorpe, Alan Rollinson, Tomoko Hasua, Margaret Capitano, Charles Kerr and Jenny Grout.

Last, but by no means least, to Gloria and Chrysa, our wives, for their constant support and encouragement—thank you.

CONTENTS

CHAPTER ONE

AN INTRODUCTION TO MARQUETRY

ABOUT THIS BOOK

This book is designed to meet the needs of the hobbyist or student of marquetry, as well as the professional furniture maker or restorer. Previous experience in the craft is not necessary since you will be guided through each technique with the help of step-by-step illustrations, showing actual 'work in progress' pictures for each design. In this way, we hope to provide full tuition of the various techniques involved in this ancient craft.

Marquetry can be described as the art and craft of making pictures and decorating furniture using exotic wood veneers. Occasionally, materials such as brass, ivory or mother-of-pearl can be used. Marquetry usually requires designs to be built up in veneer form (slices of wood cut from a log, thin enough to be cut with a craft knife), with the whole assembly glued and 'overlaid' onto a baseboard. Alternatively, marquetry designs can be assembled and then 'inlaid'. The latter requires the baseboard to be chased or routed out to a depth suitable to accommodate the inlaid design.

Our combined experience of teaching marquetry and furniture making spans over thirty years. We particularly admire the beautiful marquetry designs the master cabinetmakers of the 18th century included in their work, and it is for this reason that we have decided to give designs of this period the most detailed treatment, including fans, shells, paterae, husk swags and floral work, as well as a range of parquetry patterns.

The marquetry techniques detailed in this book provide the nucleus for the City and Guilds' qualification in 'marquetry and veneering', which in turn contributes to the Progression Award course syllabus in furniture making and restoration. The marquetry topics included in the Progression Awards stemmed from marquetry courses taught over a five-year period in two furniture-making workshops at colleges in Leeds and York. Consequently, students wishing to include marquetry in their course studies should find in the following pages the relevant theoretical references to the craft, accompanied by a range of practical exercises in the form of tutorials.

HOW TO USE THIS BOOK

The book's primary aim is to teach marquetry to students, furniture makers and restorers, and hobbyists who are new to the craft. With that in mind, we have arranged the contents in a progressive, educational order. Chapter 1 takes you through the necessary but all-important steps to learn the basic techniques. The chapter also explains, in detail, how to construct a few simple yet necessary jigs, as well as listing and advising on the pros and cons of materials such as adhesives, abrasive papers, polishes and, of course, the most important materials for this craft—the veneers. Reading, understanding and completing chapter 1 provides a foundation for success. After mastering the essential cutting exercises, you will quickly become familiar with the scalpel, allowing you to advance through the first few designs included in the marquetry tutorials given in chapter 2.

Every design is clearly illustrated in colour and explained in detail, making construction a rewarding experience. The designs are staged in order of the level of skill required, always with the assumption that you are starting out as a beginner. Our experience has shown that the demands of each tutorial are achievable without previous experience.

Chapter 5 offers the discerning cabinetmaker an opportunity to make practical and challenging furniture items. Full step-by-step plans, pictures and instructions lead you through each stage of construction. The furniture and marquetry décor are a mix of period and modern taste. A gallery tray and pier table take you back to that mid-18th century neo-classical period of English furniture making, while the jewellery box and firescreen provide more recent construction lines. Each of the four projects provides the ultimate challenge of mixing furniture making and wood-surface decoration, with eye-catching results to grace any home.

Practising marquetry and making furniture is an enjoyable experience. We trust you will gain immense satisfaction building the patterns and projects contained in this book.

If you do, your successes will be our rewards.

TOOLS AND EQUIPMENT

The tools and equipment needed in marquetry are few and inexpensive. In fact, there is only one item which costs a substantial amount—a press—and even that outlay can be greatly reduced by making your own. Both home-made and commercial presses are detailed in this section, together with the remaining off-the-shelf items that form the marqueteur's kit. A list of suppliers of tools and equipment is given near the end of the book.

FOR MARQUETRY

Cutting Mat A self-healing cutting mat offers the perfect surface for cutting veneer. The so-called A3 size is ideal for marquetry work (450 x 300 mm / 18 x 12 in). Mats are available in sizes A5, A3, A2 and A1 (the largest). Where large-sized veneers are to be worked on, it's preferable to tape two A3 mats together rather than purchase the larger A2 because two A3 mats placed end-on to each other are considerably longer than one A2.

Steel Rule A 305-mm (12-in) steel rule is essential when cutting straight lines on veneers. To prevent the rule slipping, glue a strip of sandpaper (about 240 grit) to one side of the rule. Use contact adhesive to glue the paper in place.

Geometry Tools A geometry set consisting of a small school compass and protractor, plus a 30°, 45° and 60° angle set. The latter need not be expensive items. The plastic sets found in most stationery stores are perfectly adequate.

Scalpels and Blades Figure 1 shows, from left to right, a Swann Morton 'retractable' with a No 10A; a 4-jaw chuck craft knife with 10A blade; an Ernie Ives craft knife with No 11 blade; and a Swann Morton No 3 handle with 10A blade.

Sharpening Stone A small craft stone used to regrind the back of scalpel blades. An essential tool item. See *Techniques*, p. 27.

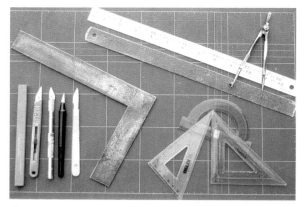

Figure 1: Basic marquetry tools

Circle Cutter For cutting perfect circles in veneers I would recommend the heavy-duty steel circle cutter. Because both compass point and cutter attachments clamp onto any steel straight edge, the radius it can cut is limitless. See *Suppliers and References*, p. 175.

Steel Straight Edge A suitable 1 metre (39 in) steel straight edge will be needed for preparing veneers when making some of the furniture projects.

Steel 90° Square Try to obtain one that has two arms, which measure at least 305 x 455 mm (12 x 18 in)—the larger the better. It will be used extensively in veneering work, for cutting material square.

Domestic Iron A domestic iron is an essential item of equipment for veneering and marquetry work.

Cutting Gauge Same as a marking gauge, but instead of a pin to mark the wood, the cutting gauge has a small blade, which cuts through the veneer. Used for making a uniform border around assembled marquetry work, it will be needed to complete some of the furniture projects, see step 2, p. 94.

Palm Sander A palm sander preferably with a vacuum attachment is an essential item. A $\frac{1}{4}$ sheet is the ideal size ($\frac{1}{4}$ of A4, or 104 x 149 mm / 4 x 6 in). The sander shown in Figure 4, page 18 is $\frac{1}{6}$th sheet size. Note the plastic skirt surrounding the sanding area. A vacuum hose plugged in at the back provides dust-free sanding.

FOR PARQUETRY

Parquetry, the technique of building geometric patterns, requires dedicated equipment to ensure accuracy of construction. A simple yet effective means of cutting repeat angles is achieved after making a small jig. This and other tools are detailed in the following section.

Gents Padsaw This ultra-thin blade, 0.20 mm (.008 in) thick, 52 teeth per inch (TPI), 12.7 mm ($\frac{1}{2}$ in) cutting depth, will saw veneers without leaving ragged edges. Used in conjunction with the mitre box (see Figure 2), this padsaw becomes an essential item for making the parquetry designs detailed in this book. See *Suppliers* on page 175.

Sliding Bevel Use this for setting the angles on the mitre box.

Tenon Saw As well as the padsaw, the tenon saw is required for sawing the first angle on the mitre box.

Mitre Box A miniature mitre box, which can be simply made to accommodate the ultra thin gents padsaw, is detailed in Figure 3.

Materials needed: softwood 75 x 25 x 225 mm (3 x 1 x 9 in) with planed surfaces to both sides; 2 strips of hardwood beading 9 x 12 x 225 mm (⅜ x ½ x 9 in). They must be perfectly flat and square.

Secure the first beading along one edge of the softwood base using PVA glue and fix one panel pin in each end. Set the second beading 50 mm (2 in) away from the first, making sure the distance is accurately maintained along its length (cut two wood blocks 50 mm / 2 in wide to use as spacers) and glue and pin into place. The mitre box is now ready for use on a number of parquetry projects.

Safety To protect your hand, place the mitre box into a bench vice before sawing cuts.

Using a 60° geometry square, set the sliding bevel to 60°. Recheck it for accuracy after tightening the bevel up—accuracy is paramount.

Figure 2: Parquetry mitre box and saw

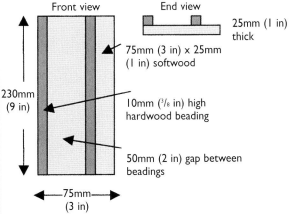

Figure 3: Mitre box dimensions

Front view | End view
25mm (1 in) thick
75mm (3 in) x 25mm (1 in) softwood
230mm (9 in)
10mm (⅜ in) high hardwood beading
50mm (2 in) gap between beadings
75mm (3 in)

Place the sliding bevel alongside the first beading, and using the tenon or dovetail saw with the blade resting against the sliding bevel, saw through both beadings and about 2 mm ($^1/_{12}$ in) into the mitre box base. The reason for using the tenon or dovetail saw for the first cut is that the gents padsaw blade is not thick enough to allow a veneer to be inserted into the cut to form the 'gate'.

Place a strip of veneer into the cut made with the tenon saw so that it protrudes above the two raised beadings. This veneer strip forms the 'gate'. To make the second mitre cut, you need to know the distance between the first and second cuts. In the case of the Louis Cube design (see p. 78) this is determined by the size you have cut the veneer strips. Using one of the strips, place it alongside the 'gate'. Using the padsaw, place the saw alongside the veneer strip and place the sliding bevel up to the saw blade, trapping the blade between the veneer and the bevel. Keeping the saw blade vertical, make a cut through both hardwood beadings, cutting all the way through to the base of the box. The box is now ready to cut 60° diamonds from your pre-prepared veneer strips.

FRETSAWING

The hand fretsaw and its blades, together with a fretsaw table, form the basic requirements for constructing the designs given in this book. Alternatively, an electrically driven fretsaw can be used if you have experience of this type of machine. Both the hand-held version and the Hegner power fretsaws are used for the exercises carried out in chapter 2.

Hand Fretsaw Consists of a U-shaped neck, called the throat, with winged clamps for holding the blade at each end. A simple handle provides a means to support the tool during use. The throat distance, measured from the blade to the turn of the neck, determines the size of veneer that can be cut. The fretsaw shown in Figure 4 has a throat depth of 310 mm (just over 12 in).

Blades Sizes are numbered by a strange method. If you remember that a number 6 is the thickest

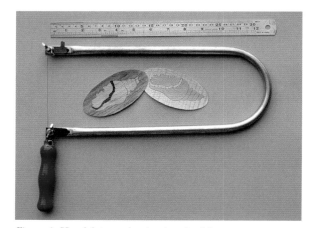

Figure 4: Hand fretsaw showing length of throat

blade and a number 6/0 is the thinnest, then the following table lists the range: 6, 5, 4, 3, 2, 1, 0, 2/0, 3/0, 4/0, 5/0, 6/0. For marquetry purposes, only the 2/0 to 6/0 range is needed. Most students advance to cutting with 6/0 blades after only a few practice sessions with the thicker blades. The gap made by a 6/0 blade is undetectable when glue is applied to the assembled joints.

Type of Blade Equally important as the size. Fretsaw blades fall into two categories, wood cutting and metal cutting. We have tried and tested both types over the last ten years and it might surprise you to know that the teeth on the wood-cutting blades are too coarse for marquetry

SIZE	THICKNESS (MM)	WIDTH (MM)	TEETH PER INCH
6/0	0.18	0.36	32
5/0	0.2	0.4	28
4/0	0.22	0.44	26.5
3/0	0.24	0.48	23.5
2/0	0.26	0.52	22
0	0.28	0.58	20.5
1	0.3	0.63	19
2	0.34	0.7	17.5
3	0.36	0.74	16
4	0.38	0.8	15
5	0.4	0.85	14
6	0.44	0.94	13.5

Figure 5: Swiss fretsaw blades

work. The metal-cutting blades, however, produce a fine, smooth cut while giving better than average blade life. The blades our students have used exclusively for the past five years are Swiss made, of hardened and tempered steel, suitable for sawing metal and other hard materials, and for use on fine veneers and marquetry (manufacturers' claim which we fully endorse). The dimensions of the Razor brand Swiss piercing saw blades made by Zona are given in figure 5. For stockist details see Suppliers' list on page 175.

Making a Fretsaw Table Using 12 mm (½ in) MDF or plywood, construct the table in Figure 6.

The table is designed to be held in a woodworking vice. The first thing that becomes apparent when using the table is that the table top, with its cut-outs, becomes invisible to the user because the veneer(s) being sawn cover up the sawing area. Therefore, keeping the saw blade within the cut-out area is achieved by feel. The cut-outs consist of a 25 mm (1 in) diameter hole for cutting out large pieces of a pattern, while a bandsaw cut made either side of this hole allows tiny pieces to be cut without them falling through the table and onto the workshop floor. Losing small pieces after cutting them out is very frustrating!

To learn how to load and use a fretsaw and the table, turn to the *Techniques* section of this chapter (pp. 34–35).

Office Stapler Used for stapling veneers together when making a fretsawing 'pad'. A standard office paper stapler is quite adequate.

Paper Adhesive A suitable paper adhesive used for sticking paper designs to a veneer. Most stationery stores sell the stick-type, rub-on adhesive, which adheres to wood as well as paper. This will be needed when making up a veneer pad.

Mini Bradawl A means of piercing tiny pin holes into the veneer pad for inserting the fretsaw blade. A standard sewing needle placed into the end of a 4-jaw chuck craft-knife holder makes an ideal miniature bradawl. If you do adopt this method, then for safety's sake make sure you push the needle into a cork when the tool is not in use.

Hammer and Screwdriver A small pin hammer will be needed to hammer the office staples flat against the veneers after fixing them through the veneer pad. To remove the staples after fret sawing, use a small electric screwdriver to prise them free of the pad.

MARQUETRY CUTTING BOARD
An essential piece of equipment for all marquetry and parquetry work. It is very simple to construct and, once made, the board will serve you for years to come. Its purpose is to provide a simple means

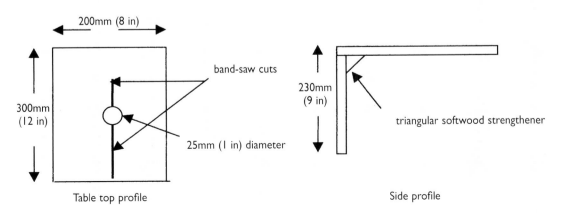

Figure 6: Dimensions for making the fretsaw table

of making repeat straight-line cuts of pre-determined size and squaring veneers accurately. Construction requires a piece of 12 mm ($\frac{1}{2}$ in) MDF or plywood, slightly bigger than an A3 cutting mat (approximately 350 x 500 mm / 14 x 20 in), plus a strip of hardwood 12 mm ($\frac{1}{2}$ in) square x 500mm (20 in) long. The strip forms a 'fixed fence' from which measured cuts can be made. See Figure 7 for dimensions.

When fixing the hardwood fence to the MDF board, it is essential that the front edge facing into the board is flat and even along its length. To check this, lay a steel straight edge up to the front edge of the strip and check for flatness. If it is bowed *even slightly*, make sure you pull it flat up to the straight edge while you glue and pin it to the board. Nearly all the projects in this book depend on this board and its raised fence for producing accurately cut veneers. Figure 8 shows our board veneered, but only because it appears many times in this book, and we wanted it to look a bit posh!

SANDSHADING KIT

Silver Sand Silver sand is the only acceptable type of sand, since other types, such as building sand, will cling to the veneers. Silver sand consists of sharp-edged granules that do not cling to each other or to the veneers. The sand can be obtained in small quantities from either garden centres or pet shops.

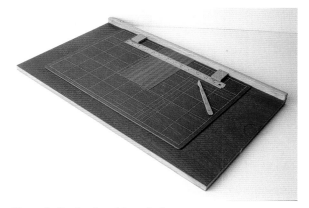

Figure 8: Cutting board in typical use

Pan A container to hold the sand should be chosen with care. First, it has to withstand heat, but more importantly it needs to transfer heat at the correct rate. The ideal container is a cast-iron frying pan. This is because iron transfers heat efficiently and will heat the sand without overheating itself. Two metals to avoid are aluminium and tin. The former is a poor conductor of heat and will result in the sand being below the correct working temperature, while tin transfers heat too quickly. Therefore, avoid using household baking tins. Steel is an acceptable metal to use.

Heater An ideal heat source is a 1-kilowatt electric hotplate. This applies heat at the correct rate for

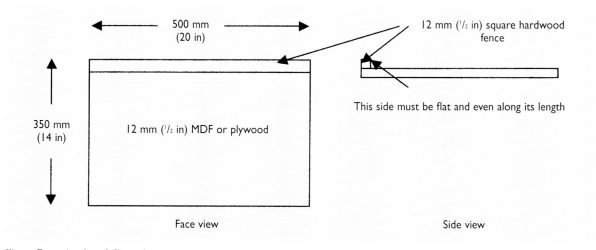

Figure 7: cutting board dimensions

constant temperature over a long period. As a temporary heat source, a gas or electric ring will suffice.

Long-Nosed Tweezers For safety reasons, a pair of tweezers is essential. The sand gets very hot—too hot to allow your fingers to touch it without suffering a nasty burn. *Always have the tweezers available at the side of the heat source.*

To learn how to sand shade veneers correctly, see the Techniques section of this chapter on pages 36–37.

Veneer Presses

A relatively expensive piece of equipment when compared with the other requirements for marquetry. Throughout this book, we only recommend the use of water-based glue, namely PVA, which needs some form of pressure while the glue sets. For the single craftsman and/or smaller colleges, construction plans for making an inexpensive bottle-jack press are given on page 167.

Hydraulic Press This is the industry choice, usually offering both cold and heated options. In veneering, where production costs demand a fast turnover, heated panel pressings can save time. For marquetry though, we generally recommend pressing without heat to prevent shrinkage, which

in turn can open the joints. Some difficult veneers, such as burrs, might require a heated press, but you should always consider the possible adverse effects of using heat. The downside to using hydraulic presses is the high cost and the floor space required.

Vacuum Press In comparison to the rest of the tools and equipment needed for marquetry work, a vacuum press looks expensive. Yet compared with the financial outlay required for woodturning or woodcarving equipment, a vacuum press does not look so costly.

The vacuum press consists of an electric pump connected by a plastic tube to a polythene bag envelope.

The veneered object is placed in the envelope and the open end sealed tight. With the pump switched on, the air in the envelope is sucked out via the tube and the pump's air outlet, thus creating a vacuum. Atmospheric pressure is applied to the outside surface of the polythene bag exerting a pressure of about 15lbs to the square inch (at sea level) to the veneered object. This equates to $^3/_4$ ton per square foot, far greater than any clamps, vices or other pressing devices found in most workshops. The figures given for calculating atmospheric pressure are always based at sea level, but the difference in operations at higher altitudes is insignificant. The running costs are negligible. A typical vacuum pump runs off a 60 watt motor and for most veneered panels the pressing time is about 1 hour.

In addition to pressing flat surfaces up to a maximum 2.4 x 1.2 m (8 x 4 ft)—the largest available bag—the vacuum press comes into its own when curved surfaces need pressing. Concave, convex or both simultaneously present no problem to the press, as the polythene bag forms itself around the object, applying equal pressure across the whole surface. This is a real advantage in veneering, because previously it was always necessary to build a matching male-to-female former (mould) to apply uniform pressure to a curved surface—the former sometimes taking longer to construct than the item itself. The

Figure 9: Long-nosed tweezers to the rescue

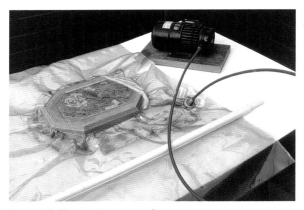

Figure 10: Vacuum press at work

picture (Figure 10) shows a veneered panel inside the vacuumed envelope. Breather fabric can be seen across the panel, linking it to the outlet tube. This is necessary in order to provide an 'air path', thus ensuring that all air is extracted from the bag to achieve maximum vacuum conditions.

Bottle-Jack Press This is an affordable press for the individual or small college. The press relies on two car bottle-jacks and a stout timber frame. The financial outlay is low compared to the two previous types of press and, apart from curved surfaces, will serve most needs for pressing moderately small to medium-sized panels. The pressure works quite simply: the two jacks apply pressure to two platens, between which the veneered panel is placed. Providing stout timbers are used in the construction, very little can go wrong and it should give many years service.

When veneers are placed in the press, it is important to use packing material (newspaper works well): firstly, to prevent the boards bonding together if glue spills; and secondly, to provide a cushion to counteract any slight unevenness in the veneer thickness.

The dimensions and construction plan for a bottle-jack press are given in the Appendix, p. 167.

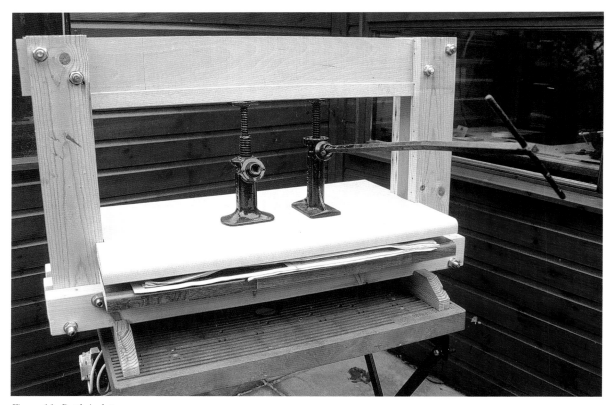

Figure 11: Bottle-jack press

MATERIALS

Like the tools, the materials required for marquetry are few and inexpensive. They essentially fall into five categories, namely tapes, adhesives, abrasives, polishes and veneers.

TAPES

Tape is used in veneering and marquetry to hold work together until a more permanent bond (glue) is applied. The tapes used fall into two distinct types, temporary tapes and semi-permanent tapes. It is important to understand the distinction between the two types.

A temporary tape is used to hold two or more pieces of veneer together, but is always removed before the assembled work is glued to a baseboard. Such tapes for marquetry are masking tape and plastic Sellotape.

A semi-permanent tape is used to hold two or more veneers together, but stays in place during the pressing process. There are two types of semi-permanent tape. The first, called veneer tape, is manufactured specifically for veneering and marquetry work and consists of white gummed paper, usually 12 or 25 mm ($\frac{1}{2}$ or 1 in) wide. The tape is applied by wetting (usually licking), which swells the paper and allows the gum to work. After being placed across two veneers, the tape is rubbed dry, causing the paper to contract, which pulls the two veneers tightly together. Removing the tape is the reverse operation: wetting the tape swells the paper, allowing the tape to be simply 'pushed' off the veneers using the end of a steel rule. For the hobbyist, a suitable alternative to veneer tape (which can be difficult to obtain) is brown parcel tape. Available from stationery stores and Post Offices, it consists of thin brown paper with gum on one side and is usually 25 mm (1 in) wide, sold in rolls of about 5 in diameter.

The second semi-permanent tape (or 'film', as it is commercially known) is bookbinding film. Some of the parquetry tutorials in this book require this film to assist construction. Like the veneer tape, only a lightweight gum is applied to the film. After pressing, the film simply peels off.

ADHESIVES

A variety of adhesives can be used in veneering and marquetry, but for all the work detailed in this book only two types of glue are required, namely PVA and cascamite (or extramite).

Understanding your glue prior to use can save many problems. Each type of glue has its advantages as well as disadvantages and it is important to understand these and to be able to apply a 'fix it' solution if something goes wrong. Glue can be very unforgiving to the user if the ground rules are not adhered to (no pun intended!).

Poly-Vinyl Acetate (PVA) This user-friendly, non-staining water-based adhesive has become the marquetry favourite, not only for gluing completed veneered assemblies to a baseboard but also for gluing individual pieces of veneer together, edge-to-edge, during construction. The window method, for instance, relies solely on PVA to keep assembled pieces together. While the glue is white in colour when applied, it becomes transparent when dried. This is an important factor in marquetry because of the multiple glue lines that are present in an assembled picture or design. It follows that since the glue is used for the construction, using it to bond the completed work to a baseboard avoids any incompatibility problems that might arise.

Its main disadvantage is that the glue is water based! At first, this may appear a surprising statement to make, but the water in the adhesive can cause a problem in two ways. Firstly, when gluing veneers edge-to-edge during assembly, only the tiniest amount of glue should be applied to the joint(s). As soon as it is applied, it should be rubbed into the joints with your finger until it disappears and dries. If you apply too much glue, the excess water from the glue will swell the veneers causing them to buckle.

The other problem is met if excess glue is applied to the baseboard or substrate. Most of the water dissipates through the fibres of the veneers during pressing. If excess glue is applied, the higher than normal water content can again swell the veneers, resulting in blisters appearing. To overcome this, apply the glue to the baseboard using a wallpaper seam roller (see Figure 1). Having poured glue onto the baseboard, roll the glue evenly across the board with the roller. No pressure is needed with the roller because the weight of the roller alone spreads the glue very evenly. Applying a thick layer of glue does not mean that you get a stronger bond; in fact, the opposite applies with PVA. The thinner the layer you apply, the stronger the bond, always providing that total coverage of the whole surface area is achieved.

You should never apply PVA glue to the completed surface of the veneer or marquetry assembly. This may seem obvious, but we have seen PVA applied to assembled veneers followed by the horror of seeing the marquetry fall to pieces on the workshop floor. Water and veneers do not mix, so as soon as PVA is spread onto the baseboard and the veneer is offered across the glued surface, you have only two or three minutes

(at the most) to position the veneer correctly before it must be placed into a press. The solution to this is illustrated in Figure 1. Hinge one edge of the veneer to the baseboard, after positioning it centrally where you want to glue it. After spreading the glue, simply flip the veneer down onto the glued surface and place it straight into the press.

The time required to press a veneer bonded with PVA adhesive in a cold press is one hour. A further 24 hours is required for the glue to cure at room temperature. The curing time is very important, because while the veneer might appear to have bonded securely after removal from a press, the glue is still soft and not strong enough to withstand the pressure of sanding. The curing also relies on exposure to air. Therefore, do not think that you can leave the veneered assembly in the press for 24 hours. This would starve the work of air and could generate the dreaded 'black spot', a fungus that forms on the glue and penetrates the veneer through to the face side. It is then impossible to remove the tiny black spots that develop across the veneers.

Even after following the above guidelines, further mishaps can sometimes occur during pressing. Very occasionally a veneer will 'bubble' during cold pressing. This can happen with burr veneers. A theory for this is that, unlike other veneers where the grain lies longitudinally along its length, burr woods are composed of 'end-grain'. This means that the water in PVA glue, which is normally absorbed by the horizontal fibres of other veneers, can pass through end-grained veneers much more easily, causing them to swell and bubble. The more open the grain, the more water is absorbed.

Where this occurs, the solution lies with a domestic hot iron. PVA allows one chance to recover from this type of problem. This is because there is still some water present in the swollen veneer, and the adhesive is still present on the surface of the baseboard. When you apply heat, two things happen: firstly, the water dissipates from the offending veneer causing it to shrink back to its normal state; and secondly, the heat

Figure 1: Spreading PVA glue onto the baseboard

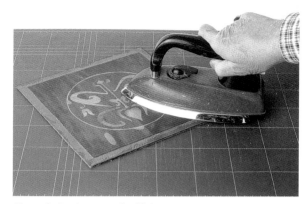

Figure 2: Ironing out a buckled veneer

softens the adhesive, providing that all-important 'grab'. After applying a hot iron for five or six seconds (set the iron to medium temperature), place a cold steel rule across the heated area and press down with hand pressure for a few seconds until the heat dissipates. The veneer should then be secure. The hot iron treatment never fails in these cases. If using a domestic iron intended for ironing clothes, protect the iron surface by placing brown paper over the veneer. Glue stains on someone's favourite item of clothing lead to problems not dealt with in this book!

Cascamite (or Extramite) A thermo-setting adhesive consisting of a white powder to which water has to be added to begin the chemical reaction. The glue, after mixing, is applied in the same way as PVA, but the setting times are much longer. For cold pressing, four hours are necessary for the glue to adhere. We have recommended using this glue to stick the two rims to the edge of the Gallery Tray, in the project in chapter 5. The stronger bond provided by this glue compared to PVA gives added strength to the assembled tray.

Scotch Glue Even today, the Italian marqueteurs use scotch glue extensively to bond veneers to the baseboard. Known as 'hammer veneering', the glue (also called 'pearl glue' or 'animal glue') is purchased in pearl form; the pearls have to be soaked in water overnight to make them swell.

Then they are heated in a metal glue pot, which is placed in an outer container full of water, electrically and thermostatically controlled to the correct temperature. Water is added to the dissolved glue to obtain the correct consistency before gluing can commence. The glue is brushed across the baseboard. A veneer hammer is used to press the veneer in place, at the same time a hot domestic iron keeps the glue workable. The term 'hammer' is most misleading, because the tool is essentially a wooden squeegee designed to be pushed along the veneer, forcing the veneer to the baseboard and the excess glue to the outer edges of the board. Scotch glue is used mainly for restoration work on antique furniture, simply because that is the type of glue first used to lay the veneers. Modern water-based glue, like PVA, cannot be used to effect repairs where scotch glue has first been used because the two glues are not compatible. There is no need for hot gluing on any of the marquetry work covered in this book.

Contact Adhesive Only as a last gasp, when all other means are exhausted, should this glue be contemplated as a means of holding down marquetry work. The only reason it is still used in this craft is that hobbyists do not have access to a press. It should be noted that this type of glue was first introduced in the late 1960s not for gluing

Figure 3: Glue pot, veneer hammer and glue pearls

wood, but for gluing plastic laminated sheets (Formica). Both surfaces have to be coated and exposure to air dries the coats in about 20 minutes. Once dry, the two surfaces are brought together and an 'impact' bond is achieved. No second chance is given; therefore, the veneer has to be correctly lined up on the baseboard without the two surfaces touching. A plastic slip-sheet is used to keep them apart while the veneer is adjusted and correctly aligned. The air is squeezed out using a narrow wallpaper roller, by starting from the centre and gradually squeezing across the veneer as the slip-sheet is slowly pulled clear.

The main reason why it is not recommended for use on marquetry work is that the glue remains soft and therefore moves with temperature changes, resulting in the polish cracking and lifting at the glue lines. You can get away with using this type of glue for single veneers where joints are not used, but for marquetry assemblies, it is well worth the effort to make a simple bottle-jack press and use PVA.

ABRASIVES

The first consideration when applying sandpaper to veneer work is the thickness of the veneer in relation to the grade of paper you intend to use. I suppose that every marqueteur has sanded through a veneer at one time or another. The trick is to understand what you are trying to achieve, then use the right materials and tools to complete the task in hand. The professional's approach is the one to observe and heed in this particular subject. They cannot afford mistakes, and must get it right every time. Hopefully, by following the guidelines given in chapter 4, you too will enjoy the same results.

Paper Grading Abrasives fall into two distinct types. One type (aluminium oxide) is for removing wood prior to commencing the polishing stage, while the second type (silicon carbide and wet or dry) is for smoothing layers of polish between coats and after coating.

Aluminium oxide sandpaper is used for removing wood and preparing a 'flat' base to

Figure 4: ¹/₆ sheet palm sander and vacuum attachment

accept a polish. The paper is available in a variety of grit sizes. To identify the grit sizes, look for the P number on the back of the paper. The lower the number the more coarse the paper. The range is P60 (the coarsest), P80, P120, P150, P180, P240, P320 and P400 (the smoothest). The red-coloured papers shown in Figure 4 are grades P80 and P120, used with an orbital palm sander to achieve the 'flat' surface.

The second type, silicon carbide and wet or dry is used for rubbing down polish after it is applied. Silicon carbide (the light grey paper in Figure 4) is available in grit sizes P220, P280, P320, P400 and P600. A special coating to the paper prevents clogging during sanding. Wet or dry (dark grey in Figure 4) consists of grades P400, P600 and P1200. Addition of water provides the anti-clogging agent.

Wirewool A very useful abrasive for the finishing process, wirewool grade 0000 is used in marquetry. It is the ideal abrasive to use when applying beeswax to a polished surface.

POLISHES

Sanding sealer consists of a cellulose-based sealant, or methylated-spirit-based (shellac) sealant, each containing either French chalk or pumice powder. The chalk or powder separates from the polish when not in use; therefore, it is very important to thoroughly shake and stir the mixture prior to use. When applied to veneers, the sealer acts as a base foundation for

Figure 5: Finishing materials

subsequent finishes to lie on. One or two coats are normally sufficient as a basecoat, if other finishing materials are to be applied afterwards.

Use cellulose sealer if a corresponding cellulose-based polish is to follow. Use shellac if spirit-based polish follows.

French Polish This is applied to furniture after application of shellac sanding sealer. French polish can be applied by a 'mop', but better finishes are achieved by application with a polisher's rubber (known as a mouse in the US).

Polyurethane Polish This is used where a tough finish or a water barrier is necessary. The polish is available in matt, satin or gloss finishes. The satin finish gives marquetry work a classic appearance. Three coats are usually applied, each coat being rubbed back with silicon carbide paper and 0000 wire wool. It dries very hard and is ideally suitable to furniture items where durability is required. Make sure you use the 'clear varnish' brand, which both dries transparent and produces a finish that is slightly mellow. This can be very attractive on certain furniture projects, as it gives a classic aged appearance.

Waxes Good quality beeswax adds a further protection to furniture. We have all witnessed the effects of water spillage on furniture where no wax polish is present. When water spills on wood protected with wax the water sits on the wax, unable to penetrate into the wood. Renaissance wax provides a tough finish, with the added benefit of not showing fingers marks, making the product ideal for items that receive the human touch, such as tables, trays and jewellery boxes.

VENEERS

Traditional veneers such as mahogany, walnut, oak and ash, together with the full range of burr woods, still dominate British furniture design. Encouragingly, cherry and yew woods have become popular in the last fifteen years. During the same period, a resurgence of traditional wood-veneered 'fitted furniture units' has replaced the Formica, plastic laminated versions of the 1960s and 1970s, resulting in high-quality natural wood-surfaced units, made for kitchens and bedrooms in our homes.

WORLD SHORTAGE

Sadly, because of deforestation of the world's rain forests, some exotic woods have either declined in quantity or become totally unavailable. Strict import/export controls have forced manufacturers to look at alternative sources and new innovations. America is actively opening new forest management programmes to reproduce timbers that have become threatened species, and already the yield from these projects has made a major impact on our imports.

Additionally, scientific development has seen the introduction of commercial 'Reconstructed Real Wood Veneers' (or multi-laminar veneers as they are also known). These veneers are today being used alongside their natural equivalents in the fitted-furniture industry. Reconstructed real-wood veneers are manufactured from three basic timbers: poplar, obeche and koto, chosen because of their softness, light figureless colour and large open pores, which allow dyes to permeate the full thickness of the veneers. The felled logs are first trimmed along the length to form a uniform rectangular block of wood, which is then sliced into veneers. A selected veneer from another 'naturally' grown timber is scanned into a computer, which reads the colour and grain pattern of that veneer and passes the data to the processor. The processor calculates the correct dye to copy the veneer's colour and also works out the grain and figure structure from the scanned sample. In turn, the data is passed onto the workshop to prepare a mould to match the pattern exactly. Each sliced veneer is injected with coloured dye. After this process, the veneers are glued together and compressed into the mould under high pressure. To produce straight-grained types, sheets of dyed veneers are glued and pressed into flat moulds that are then turned on their side and sliced. To produce a wider stripe the block is turned at an angle before slicing—the wider the angle, the wider the stripe. To produce a crown type figure, a mould is built to the shape and contours of the sample and after the sliced veneers are again dyed, glued and pressed into the shape, the pressed block is planed flat, then sliced to produce a crowned figured leaf. The end product means that every

veneer sliced from the log is identical in colour and grain pattern and matches the characteristics of the chosen species. Figure 6 illustrate the processing stages.

The benefits of reconstructed real-wood veneers are many, including less impact on the environment and the world's ecosystem and less devastation of natural rain forests. Each batch of veneers produced is exactly the same, in colour and figure—something that could never be produced from two different trees of the same species. Four examples of reconstructed real wood veneers are given in Figure 7. The first three have a bird's-eye figure, while the fourth represents rosewood.

Of the 70,000 species of trees grown on our planet, only about 350 are available commercially. That number has greatly decreased since the mid-1970s, mainly for the reasons already discussed. Luckily, in marquetry and veneering terms, most

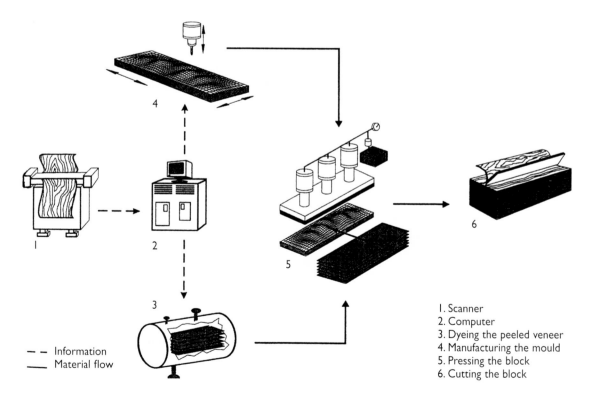

– – Information
—— Material flow

1. Scanner
2. Computer
3. Dyeing the peeled veneer
4. Manufacturing the mould
5. Pressing the block
6. Cutting the block

Figure 6: Processing stages for making reconstructed real wood veneers

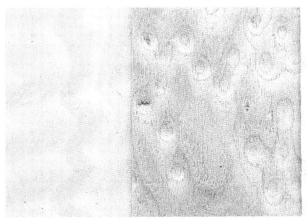

Figure 7: Samples of reconstructed real-wood veneers

of the popular species are still available and, where not, suitable alternatives have now taken their place.

KNOW YOUR WOODS

One quick, sure way to learn the different species of veneer is to start a veneer album. Each 'find' makes you look up reference books to find its name(s), place(s) of origin, its general description, its uses, plus any peculiarities the species has to offer. You will be amazed how absorbing you will find the exercise and, before you know it, you will have collected over fifty species without even seeming to try. The hardest and most complex aspect to wrestle with is the common name. Some species carry many common names. Some carry misleading names— perhaps chosen for marketing reasons. A typical example is Australian Silky Oak (*cardwellia*

Figure 8: Veneer albums in A4 ring binders

sublimis), so named because it has a silver ray figure, similar to that in the true oak (*quercus*). Fortunately, every tree has its unique scientific or botanical name, which cannot be changed no matter where you are in the world. Another example that can easily cause confusion is mahogany, where the common name refers to two distinct trees:

FAMILY	GENUS	SPECIES	COMMON NAME
Meliaceae	*Swietenia*	*macrophylla*	mahogany
Meliaceae	*Khaya*	*ivorensis*	mahogany

While both the above species originate from the same family, Meliaceae, we know from studying the cellular structure of woods that the true mahogany is from the genus *Swietenia*, whose origin is Central and South America. Other physical properties such as colour, density, grain, figure and sometimes odour are also useful identifiers. The cellular structure, colour, grain and figure of *Khaya*, when examined with or without a microscope, differs to *Swietenia*, and therefore we know that *Khaya*, whose origin is Tropical Africa, is not a true mahogany. Despite this, both species, across the world, share the common name. There are many, many other examples of woods whose common names bear little, if any, resemblance to the timbers they are attached to. Suffice it to say that it is much more fun to find them out for yourself.

FROM TREE TO VENEER

One living tree can offer a variety of different figured woods, depending on which part of the tree the wood is cut from and what type of cut is applied. Naturally, the trunk of the tree offers the main source of timber but occasionally, outcropped growths at the foot of the tree and in the root system provide the much sought-after burr (burl in the US) woods. Burrs are growths which occur either from parasitic activity within the tree, or induced by forest management when the plant is a tiny sapling. As side shoots (small branches) try to develop, the shoots are removed to encourage the main trunk to develop. Consequently, over a number of years, the tree develops a growth protruding from the trunk at ground level. When this growth is sliced into, to produce veneers, it reveals a mass of decorative swirls and knots indicating where growth has been suspended or where parasites have been active. This timber, unlike the main trunk area, has no longitudinal grain direction but consists wholly of end-grain. Burrs are highly sought after for cabinetwork. Needless to say, they provide the perfect background veneer to show off marquetry work and should be used as often as possible.

SLICING LOGS INTO VENEER

Modern mechanisation and technology can produce veneers thin enough to allow us to cut almost all of them with a standard craft knife. Prior to this, logs had to be sawn to produce veneers, resulting in a thickness (3 mm, or $^1/_8$ in) unusable for knife work. Today, on the other hand, veneers are available in thicknesses ranging from 0.7 to 0.9 mm, equivalent to $^1/_{40}$ in to $^1/_{28}$ in respectively. Veneers are sliced from the log in many ways, each producing a pattern so distinct in appearance and texture that it is difficult to imagine two veneers, cut two different ways, originating from the same species. A selection of the cuts, and the patterns that emerge, is illustrated on the following pages.

CURL, CROTCH OR FLAME VENEER

Any of the three names given above describes this veneer. It is a product of the tree where two branches split from the main trunk area, producing a 'Y' shape. Mahogany curl is used extensively to decorate the centre of panels on high-class cabinetwork. It is not the easiest of veneers to work with, particularly in large panels, having a tendency to split and buckle because the grain direction splits at the crotch of the two branches, causing internal stresses in the veneer. It is usual practice to soften the veneer first, by wetting and placing it under weights between sheets of paper for a few days, prior to cutting. Even after cutting, it pays to keep it under pressure until ready for mounting and pressing to groundwork.

CROWN CUT

Crown cut veneers offer the best figure arrangement. Figure 9 shows the cut slicing through the growth rings. First, the log is sawn down the centre to provide a 'flat' to enable the trunk to be clamped to a 'stay block' while the knife, set at veneer thickness (0.7 or 0.9 mm), slices through the trunk under the control of a pressure head.

The resulting veneer displays sapwood at both edges (in some species) and a very attractive crowned figure rising in the shape of a 'cathedral' at the centre of the leaf. Figure 9 shows American black walnut (*juglans nigra*) veneer, with the distinctive cathedral shape in the centre of the leaf.

ROTARY CUT

Rotary cut timbers were first used for making plywood, being cut much thicker than veneers. Rotary cutting is achieved by placing the log on a revolving lathe. A stationary knife slices a continuous sheet of veneer, like dispensing a paper roll. The continuous sheet is then cut into pre-selected panel sizes.

(*Macroberlinia brazzavillensis*), shown in Figure 11, are products of this type of cut.

IDENTIFYING THE 'FACE' SIDE

All veneers have two sides, one the right side (the face) and one the wrong side (the reverse or check side).

There are two ways to identify which is the face side and which is the reverse side of a veneer. It is important to know this because the two opposing sides have different characteristics and appearance. For instance, parquetry patterns depend on repeat pieces all having the same size, colour and appearance throughout the assembly. If one piece is reversed and all the others are face-side up, the change in either colour tone or characteristic can stand out like a beacon, spoiling the effect you are trying to achieve.

The reason why the characteristic and colour changes is because when you turn a veneer over the grain is laying at a different angle than before, and due to the angle of the light hitting the surface (light refraction), the veneer looks noticeably different. This on its own is not enough to identify which side is the face, but if you look again you will notice that the face side is smoother and appears slightly dome-shaped, even though the veneer is perfectly flat. Conversely, the reverse side is coarser and flat, with the surface looking almost hollowed out.

The other method of distinguishing the two sides is used where medium to large leaves are at hand. By holding a veneer at arm's length along one side of the leaf, so that the grain is running 90° to your arm, the veneer will droop downwards quite significantly if the face side is pointing upwards. The downward droop is much reduced if the reverse side is pointing upwards. This is because the check side (reverse grain direction) provides more stability to the leaf.

MATCHING LEAVES

Veneers are stacked and retained in the order in which they are sliced off the log. This is to retain

Figure 9: Crown cut

American black walnut

Figure 10: Rotary cut

Bird's-eye maple

Figure 11: Quarter cut

Zebrano

Typical rotary cut veneers include the well-known birds-eye maple (see Figure 10), kevasinga (bubinga tree), masur birch, obeche, koto and pommelle (sepele tree).

QUARTER CUT

The log is cut into equal quarters along its length and sliced across the growth rings as illustrated. This produces a distinctive stripe figure. Sepele (see veneer samples, p. 24) and zebrano

VENEER SAMPLES

SYCAMORE

(*Acer pseudoplatanus*)

Origin: Central Europe and UK

Sandshades perfectly

ROCK MAPLE

(*Acer saccharum*)

Origin: Canada and Eastern USA

Sandshades very well

MAGNOLIA

(*Magnolia grandiflora*)

Origin: USA

Sandshades very well

BOXWOOD

(*Buxus sempervirens*)

Origin: Europe and South America (*gossypiospermum praecox*)

Used for making inlay lines, stringings and so on

Sandshades: Yes

SEPELE

(*Entandrophragma cylindricum*)

Origin: West and East Africa

Used for crossbanding because of its striped figure.

POMMELLE

(*Entandrophragma cylindricum*)

Origin: West and East Africa

Rotary-cut version of the sepele tree

MAHOGANY

(South American, *Swietenia macrophylla*)

Origin: Honduras, Brazil

POPLAR

(*populus spp*)

Origin: Europe and Canada

Makes reconstructed real-wood veneers. Sandshades: Yes

OBECHE

(*Triplochiton scleroxylon*)

Origin: West Africa

Makes reconstructed real-wood veneers

Sandshades: Yes

ANINGERIA

(*aningeria spp*)

Origin: West Africa

Known as anègre

Sandshades: Yes

BURRS (BURLS)

MADRONA BURR

(*Arbutus menziesii*)

Origin: Canada and USA

Sandshades: Yes

MAPLE BURR

(*Acer saccharum*)

Origin: Canada and USA

Sandshades: Yes

ASH BURR

(*Fraxinus excelsior*)

Origin: Europe

Sandshades: Yes

VAVONA BURR

(*Sequoia sempervirons*)

Origin: California, USA

From the giant Sequoia tree

MYRTLE BURR

(*Umbellularia californica*)

Origin: USA

POPLAR BURR

(*populus spp*)

Origin: Europe and USA

Sandshades: Yes

the repeat of grain and figure pattern that is inherent in each veneer. As the log is sliced, each pattern 'slips' slightly as the veneers increase or decrease in width depending on the type of cut that has been made.

It is very important that the veneers are kept in the order they are cut, so that matching leaves can be achieved when veneering furniture panels. Book-matching is where two identical leaves are opened up like a book: as one veneer is turned over to the reverse side to produce a mirror image of the first veneer kept face side up. The reversed veneer also takes on a new appearance, due to the grain lying at a different angle and the effect of light refraction. Over the past decades, cabinetmakers have made good use of this phenomenon by using both reversed and face-sided veneers on opposite panels of cabinets to add an additional feature.

Quarter matching involves four identical veneers where two of the four veneers are reversed and the other two retained face-side up. Italian marqueteurs make great use of quarter matching by making up a pad of four matching leaves (usually a burr) and adding four leaves of a plain white veneer (such as sycamore). One quarter of a marquetry design is pasted to the top of the pad and the pattern is fretsawed out. After assembling the fretwork, the four leaves are opened up in book form to reveal a complete match of the background veneer as well as the complete marquetry pattern. Many of their table tops and cabinet panels are decorated using this advanced technique.

TECHNIQUES

USING THE KNIFE

Of all the techniques associated with this craft, use of the knife is the most important. To this end, it is equally important that you spend some considerable time both reading about the tool and practising the cutting exercises detailed below.

Most veneers these days are sliced to thickness between 0.7 and 0.9 mm, which means that most are capable of being cut with a scalpel or similarly sharp craft knife. The ultimate aim, when cutting veneers to shape into each other, is to achieve—as nearly as possible—a perfect joint.

BEVELLED BLADE

The first consideration when using the knife is the two-sided bevel of the blade. As the blade is pressed into a veneer, the shape of the bevel leaves a 'V'-shaped groove, leaving a wider gap on the cutting side than on the reverse side, as shown in Figure 1.

Some marqueteurs reverse the design and cut from the reverse side of the veneer, so that when the assembly is turned over the design is the right way round and the gap made by the knife is at its narrowest.

This approach can create problems when the assembly is mounted to a groundwork (the panel onto which the veneers are glued) and you begin to sand the veneers. When you sand the reverse side you are reducing the veneer thickness at the point where the knife cut is already thinnest, revealing the levels at which it is progressively wider. Conversely, if you sand from the cutting side you are sanding towards the progressively narrower part of the cut, and therefore improving the finished appearance. We always work from the face side.

THE WINDOW METHOD

The window method of construction consists of cutting a shape out of one veneer, which is called the 'window', and filling the shape with another veneer, called the 'insert'. Figure 2a illustrates the 'V'-shaped sides of the window caused by the bevelled blade and the corresponding, but reversed, 'V'-shaped sides of the insert. It is clear from the drawing that the insert is best 'inserted' from the reverse side of the window. Figure 2b shows the resulting gap on the face side, which reduces when the veneers are sanded.

CUTTING TECHNIQUES

There are five types of cuts used when cutting veneers. These are: Straight, Sweep, Score, Step and Stab.

Knowing which cut to use and where to use it is the key to achieving good joints. This section should be read thoroughly and the accompanying exercises carried out until you become totally familiar with the knife, its blade and the types of

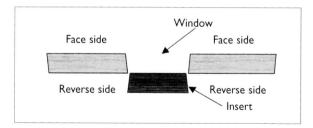

Figure 2a: Always insert from the reverse side

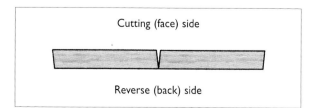

Figure 1: Cut resulting from bevelled blade

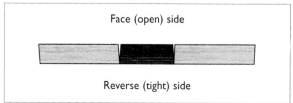

Figure 2b: Resulting gap on face side

cut. First, however, we need to discuss the choice of knife and how to maintain it.

CHOICE OF BLADE

There are endless types of knife handle available and the choice is a matter of personal taste. Choose the one that feels comfortable in your hand. Swann Morton industrial blades of sizes 10A and 11 are the most suitable types for this craft. The 10A is wide and short and the 11 is narrow and long. Both are the same thickness.

Retaining a sharp point on the tip of the blade is essential. All you need to do is reproduce a new point and this is achieved by rubbing the back of the blade along the surface of the sharpening stone, backwards and forwards, to create a groove in the stone. In a matter of a few strokes, a new point will be formed.

Each of the five techniques is illustrated in the following two exercises—in the window method and in circle cutting—which aim to simulate the problems you will encounter when building marquetry and parquetry designs. To undertake them you will need the following tools and materials:

Scalpel or equivalent craft knife
Masking tape (plus possibly veneer tape)
Steel rule
Compass and pencil
Two contrasting squares of veneer, about 150 mm (6 in) on each side
PVA glue
Sharpening stone
Self-healing cutting mat

Cutting straight lines is generally performed with the aid of a steel rule. The knife is drawn down the veneer, making a sweeping cut. Use your non-cutting hand to hold the steel rule firmly in place, making sure your fingers are behind the edge that the knife will run along. The first cut must always be a light one. This makes the initial groove in the veneer. Second and third cuts can be firmer because the initial groove keeps the knife on line.

Now try cutting a straight-sided shape (a triangle, say) to create a window, into which we can insert another veneer. Draw a triangle onto a piece of veneer, with each side about 50 mm (2 in) long (see overleaf).

Figure 3: Shaping a new point to the back of a scalpel blade

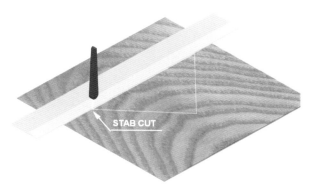

1 Place the rule along the line to be cut. Make a vertical stab cut at the end of the line that is nearest your body. This forms a registration mark to prevent the knife cutting beyond the line.

2 Angle the scalpel blade at about 2° to the vertical and about 45° to the horizontal. Place the scalpel at the end furthest away from your body and draw the blade very lightly towards you in a light, slow, sweeping motion. As you reach the end of the cut, the blade will drop into the stab mark, signalling you to stop.

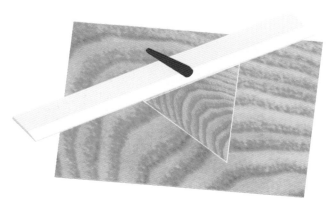

3 Place the knife back at the start of the cut again and this time press harder. The groove you created on the first cut will now hold the blade in place. Repeat the action until you cut through the veneer. Do not take your hand off the rule until you complete the cut.

4 Turn the veneer to allow you to cut the second side of the triangle. Always keep your hands in the same position throughout cutting. Cut the second and third sides in the same way as the first.

Stab cut

5 You have now cut out a 'window'. The next step is to insert another veneer to fill the window, making a perfect fit. Welcome to 'The Window Method'!

If a veneer is open grained, or brittle and likely to split during cutting, a useful tip is to place strips of veneer tape onto the face side of the 'insert' veneer, to protect it. It also has the added benefit of making the scored line stand out clearly. The tape can be left in place until the assembled panel is pressed to its groundwork.

6 Position another veneer behind the window, holding it in place with two tabs of masking tape. Score the insert along all three sides where the two veneers meet. Place the knife at the point nearest to your body and angle it at about 2° to the vertical. Move the knife forward about 10 mm (³/₈ in) then draw it back towards yourself, making a light score mark into the veneer. It is necessary to score the veneer without cutting through it. Move the knife forward another 10 mm and again draw it back until it drops into the score line you made on the previous cut. As you get to each point of the triangle, make a vertical stab cut to highlight the points.

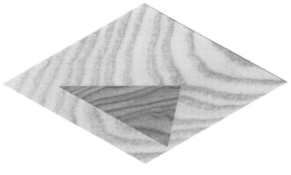

7 Remove the insert from the window and place it on the cutting mat. Starting at the lowest left-hand corner, make step cuts through the scored line (shown in red for clarity) by holding the knife vertical to the surface. Move the knife forward 10 mm from the corner and draw it towards you, cutting into the scored line. Move forward another 10 mm and repeat, until the knife drops into the previous cut. Progress forward like this and keep turning the veneer as you cut around the piece until the insert pops free. Use of the steel rule is optional.

8 Place the insert into the window from the reverse side and apply a few drops of PVA glue to the joints. Rub the glue until it is dry.

CIRCLES

Cutting and inserting a perfect circle is a useful exercise because it teaches control of the knife throughout the process. The aim is to complete the circle as accurately as it was initially drawn with your compass (see below).

FRETSAWING

A big advantage of fretsawing is that any veneer can be cut with ease. Tropical hardwood veneers, which are always the most beautiful, can be used to good effect. Cutting intricate shapes into rosewoods, tulipwood, satinwood, African ebony, wenge etc., is usually avoided in knife work, but they present no problem to the fretsaw. For furniture work, it opens up a whole new and exciting world, offering the craftsman a totally free choice in the type of veneer he or she wishes to use.

THE PAD METHOD

A pad is simply a number of veneers held together with pins or staples, with a fretsaw design pasted to the top leaf. The design, in the form of a line drawing, dictates the paths which the fretsaw takes to saw out the shapes. Once all the shapes have been cut out, removing the pins or staples separates the pad and two contrasting designs can be constructed. The following paragraph explains why two designs are obtained.

The fretsaw designs in this book consist of what are called positive/negative designs. This means that the sawn image appears in two forms, both the required colour (positive) and the reverse colour (negative). Building up a veneer pad to make such a design requires four veneers. Of these, one veneer is for the design and one for the background (these two are called the sandwich). To protect the sandwich, the third and fourth veneers are placed above and below it (these two are called the wasters). The bottom waster takes the kerf of the saw as the fretsaw blade leaves the pad, tearing the waster as the saw leaves the wood, while the waster above the sandwich has the paper design pasted onto it.

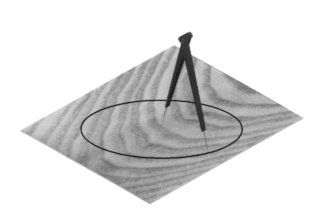

1 Draw a 50mm (2 in) circle on the veneer using your compass.

2 Make short step cuts by moving the knife forward 10mm (¹/₂ in) at a time and drawing it towards you as you cut through the line. Cut directly on the line, not either side of it. Make light cuts on the first circuit round the circle, followed by heavier cuts on second/third circuits. Keep moving the workpiece and cut till the window pops out.

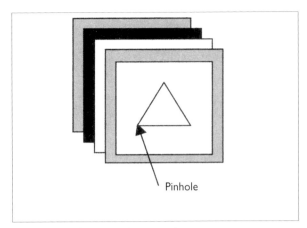

Figure 4a: Making up a fretsaw pad

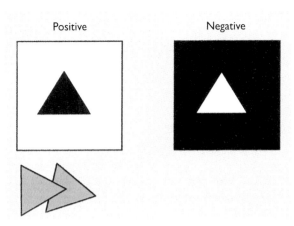

Figure 4b: Assembling the sawn designs

For illustration purposes (see Figure 4a), let us make our sandwich from one black and one white veneer. Surround the sandwich with two red veneers as wasters, one above and the other below. A paper design (a triangle) is pasted onto the top waster, and the pad of veneers is stapled together (not illustrated). A pinhole is then made into a convenient part of the design, and the fretsaw blade is inserted through the pinhole from the back of the pad to cut out, in this case, an equilateral triangle. Removing the staples separates the pad, and Figure 4b shows the four triangles—the two red wasters can now be discarded. The black triangle fits into the white

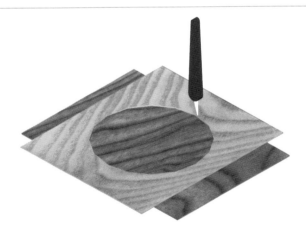

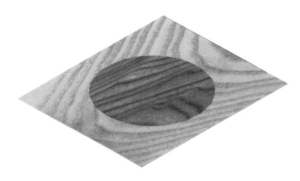

3 Tape a veneer behind the window with masking tape. Place the knife into the joint where the insert veneer meets the window. Hold the knife at a 2° angle to the verticle. move forward 10mm ($^1/_2$ in) and draw the knife back to *score* the insert veneer. Repeat the scored cut around the circle.

 Place the insert veneer onto your cutting mat (not shown). Now hold the knife vertical to the surface. Cut through the scored line with short *step* cuts no longer than 10mm ($^1/_2$ in). Short cuts keep you in control of the line you are cutting. Move forward and draw the knife back towards you as before, as you move round the scored line. The insert will eventually pop free.

4 Turn the window veneer over and place the insert into the hole from the back. Put the thinnest drops of PVA glue around the joint and rub it in with your fingers until it disappears and is dry.

 Turn the assembly over and inspect your efforts. If you have gaps—as you almost certainly will when you first start—begin again, until you develop the technique. Practice makes perfect.

veneer, while the white triangle fits into the black veneer—hence the two designs. These alternative designs are referred to as positive and negative. Depending on your needs, both can be used, or just one. Furniture makers in the 17th century were quick to spot the positive/negative potential and put it to good effect. Consequently many antique examples exist from that period onwards. Examples where decorative fretwork is present on furniture might show the positive image on, say, a door on one half of a cabinet, with the exact opposite, negative image appearing on the adjacent door.

PREPARING THE PAD

Continuing with the 'two-colour design' arrangement, let us explain how to make up a veneer pad to make one of the designs detailed in chapter 2: the patera. Follow these guidelines carefully and you will fretsaw a patera successfully.

Select two veneers to form the sandwich. Figure 5 illustrates magnolia (second left) and sycamore (third left) with any two veneers for wasters (left and right). The pattern of the patera is ready for pasting to the pad when assembled. Always use two veneers that have a strong visual contrast; the pattern could become lost in the background if the colours chosen are too similar.

Cut the two sandwich veneers about 2.5 cm (1 in) larger (all round) than needed. Make sure that the longest measurement does not exceed the length of the throat of the fretsaw frame.

Figure 6: Taping and stapling the pad

Using broad brown paper parcel tape (approximately 50 mm/2 in wide), wet the gummed tape and stick it to the face side of the two sandwich veneers. Taping is very important, because you are going to be fretsawing across short grains for some of the design. Without tape to strengthen the veneer, breakages will certainly occur and ruin the work. You do not need to tape the wasters.

Place the four veneers together to form a pad. It is usual to have the grain of both the sandwich veneers travelling in the same direction. If your design is a rectangle or, as here, an ellipse, the grain normally lies along the longest length. If the design is vertical, then usually the grain runs vertically. If the design is circular, usually the grain runs horizontal to the shape. The two sandwich veneers should have the tape side facing you and should be surrounded above and below by the two wasters. Use an office stapler to punch a staple in each of the four corners. Hammer the pins of the staples flat on the base of the pad so that the pad can be manoeuvred with ease on the fretsaw table. Use a stick-type rub-on paper adhesive to paste the paper design centrally on the top waster. If the design is a circle or ellipse, place more staples around the outer circumference of the area (see Figure 6). You can place staples into the design area as long as you place them where the figured background veneer will eventually reside. Do not under any circumstance place staples in the white veneer

Figure 5: Materials for a 'patera' pad

that depicts the design, because the staple holes will show in the finished work.

For centuries, cabinetmakers have chosen highly decorative veneers as a background to complement their fretsawn designs. Veneers such as rosewood, tulipwood, kingwood and all the best-figured burr (burl) woods are found. The first reason for using these types of veneer was for appearance, but the second and technical reason was to disguise the nails they used to hold the pads together. The Italian marqueteurs adopt the very same approach today, which is why a visit to their workshops is the nearest you will get to witnessing these centuries-old techniques.

MAKING PINHOLES

You have to decide where to start fretsawing. Some designs do not need any thinking about, whereas others require a great deal of study to work out the correct sequence of cuts. The first things to look for are the so-called 'island' pieces, which are small pieces of the design residing within the boundary of a larger piece. In these cases, the island piece(s) must always be cut out first. The island piece in the patera is the oval in the centre of the design. This must be cut out first because it then allows access to the 12 petals that surround the oval. An effective tool for making the pinhole is a craft knife, with a 4-jaw chuck, which will tighten onto a sewing needle. It makes an ideal miniature bradawl. An important safety tip: if you do adopt this method, for safety's sake, push the needle into a wine cork when the tool is not in use (see Figure 7). Pierce a hole somewhere along the line of the inner oval shape. Thread a 6/0 (or 2/0 if still learning) Swiss metal cutting blade from the back of the pad and connect the blade to the fretsaw jaw. Figure 7 shows a Hegner motorized fretsaw being used, but a hand-held fretsaw on a home-made fretsaw table will produce just the same job.

Figure 7: Fretsawing with a Hegner machine. Note the mini bradawl in the cork

LOADING A BLADE INTO A HAND-HELD FRETSAW

First of all, it is best to load a blade while sitting down. A blade should first be inserted into the clamp at the handle end of the fretsaw, with the teeth of the blade facing towards the handle. The teeth of the Swiss-type blades are so small that you will have to run a finger along the blade to determine the direction they are facing. Insert about 12 mm ($\frac{1}{2}$ in) of the blade into the clamp, making sure the blade points towards the opposite clamp and is not pointing upwards or downwards (one of the main reasons for breakages during loading). Tighten the wing nut by hand, as tight as you can get it. Thread the blade through the pinhole from the back of the pad. Pull on the unclamped end of the blade in one hand while you slide the pad down the length of the blade towards your body until it touches the handle end of the frame. With the pad resting on your thighs for support, and the handle of the saw pressed into your stomach/chest, use the forefinger and thumb to hold the free end of the blade and wrap the other three fingers of the

Figure 8: Loading a blade, sitting position

same hand around the frame of the saw. Pull the frame towards you and offer the blade into the far clamp so that 12 mm ($\frac{1}{2}$ in) of blade enters the clamp. Hold the tension while you use your other hand to tighten the wing nut, hand tight. Figure 8 illustrates the technique.

Finally, support the loaded pad in one hand while you move the saw with the other into the cut-out on your fretsaw table. Once in place, pull the saw blade through the pinhole and begin fret sawing.

Figure 9: Hand fretsawing on a homemade fretsaw table

USING THE HAND FRETSAW

There is one golden rule that must be applied when fretsawing a pad of veneers. Keep the saw vertical to the pad being sawn. If you allow the saw to tilt at an angle to the pad, you will produce a bevelled cut through the pad, resulting in either loose-fitting joints, or no fit at all. Figure 10 illustrates cuts made through the pad of four veneers. With a 90° cut each veneer will fit into any of the other three veneers in the pack. The tilted cuts, however, result in either a loose or overtight fit.

The 90° cuts still leave the problem of the gap made by the thickness of the saw blade. We have been able to eliminate this by using the right blade type and size (see the section on *Tools and Equipment* earlier in this chapter). Using a 6/0 (smallest size) metal cutting blade, the gap, once assembled and filled with PVA glue, is totally invisible.

A FEW SAWING TIPS

Vertical Sawing To help you keep the saw vertical, try to saw with your elbow tucked into the side of your body. This in turn keeps your upper arm still, which helps you to concentrate on maintaining the saw in the vertical mode.

Sharp Bends For hand sawing, when you come to a sharp turn or point in the design, pull slightly back on the saw, so that the back of the blade rubs on the pad. Keep the sawing action going while you turn the pad with your other hand. Once you have completed the turn, push forward on the saw and continue cutting along the line. For machine sawing, simply stop pushing and turn the piece around, against the back of the blade.

Going Off-line If you go off-line, do not stop and try to change direction immediately. Instead, gradually return to the cutting line in a smooth 'unnoticed' correction.

Sawing Very Tiny Pieces When sawing very tiny pieces (so small that they would drop through the 25 mm/1 in diameter hole in the handmade fretsaw table), carry out the fretwork above the bandsaw-cut portion of the table. In this way, more support will be given to the tiny piece, and you will be able to recover it from the pad when it is cut free. For machine sawing, use the special insert that comes with the machine that has a tiny hole for the blade to move through, but not big enough for sawn pieces to drop through.

Accent Lines These are artistic lines which, in fretsawn designs, should be cut before a piece is removed from the pad. For example, suppose you were cutting a petal of a floral design. Naturally, this would consist of one piece—the shape of a petal. However, to give the petal artistic animation, the veins of the petal are represented as 'blind cuts', better known as accent lines. The lines are drawn up the centre of a petal, but stop

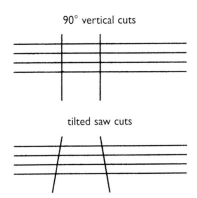

Figure 10: The importance of vertical sawing

Figure 11: Dark accent lines on each petal

short before reaching the outer edges. This requires fretsawing up each vein, turning the blade 360° and sawing back down the vein. After this, the petal can be sawn from the design. After the design is assembled and before it is glued to a baseboard, a darkened grain filler is squeezed into the gap, from the back of the assembly, giving the petal the required artistic effect. Veneer tape applied to the face side of the petal prevents the grain filler from escaping. Figure 11 illustrates the accent lines, or veins running up the centres of each petal and down either side of the centre from the top of each petal. To ensure the lines were visible, a 2/0-size blade was used for cutting out the patera design.

SANDSHADING

Perhaps the most ancient but also most important technique used in creating marquetry images is the art of sandshading—and it is indeed an art, since scorching veneers in hot sand allows the marqueteur to create an artistic image just as a painter might do with a brush. Sometimes also referred to as 'animation', sandshading veneers has been a vital part of the craft from a very early age. English cabinetmakers of the 18th century used the technique constantly, by sandshading the many motifs, such as fans, urns, shells and sunburst paterae, which adorned their furniture. A number of these motifs form the nucleus of the tutorials within this book, so it is important to understand how the technique is performed and the type of equipment needed.

THE TECHNIQUE

It is very important to achieve the correct level of shading if the ideal artistic image is to be realized. If you undershade the veneer, you might find the scorching is removed during the finishing process, leaving no effect at all. If you overshade the veneer, it will look burnt and unsightly and destroy the effect you are aiming for. The perfect shaded effect is where it is barely obvious that sandshading has occurred, yet the three-dimensional image is present. Subtlety and uniformity are the two effects you should aim to

achieve. The following tips will help you learn the skills and improve your technique.

Cut ten strips of sycamore or maple veneer about 100 mm (4 in) long and 25 mm (1 in) wide, with the grain running down the length of the strips. Heat up the silver sand, which should be about 25 mm thick across the pan base. It generally takes about 20 minutes to heat up sand to the required temperature, using a 1-kilowatt heater and a cast-iron pan. (See the section on *Tools* earlier in this chapter for details.)

SAFETY PRECAUTIONS

The sand needs to be very hot to burn veneers and you will need to hold your hand very close to the sand in order to insert and remove the veneer strips. Should a veneer fall over and lie flat on the bed of sand, do not attempt to pick it up with your fingers! Touching the hot sand with your fingers could cause a painful burn. Instead, always have a pair of long-nosed tweezers at hand and use them to recover the veneer. You should also ensure that the heater and pan of sand are positioned in the workplace clear of other combustible materials. Finally, always disconnect the heat source when you have finished shading.

TEST FOR TEMPERATURE

Take a strip of veneer and hold it between forefinger and thumb so that one edge of the veneer is facing the bed of sand. Push the veneer into the sand without letting your fingers touch

Figure 12: 1-kilowatt heater, iron pan and silver sand

Figure 13: Create a raised flat plateau

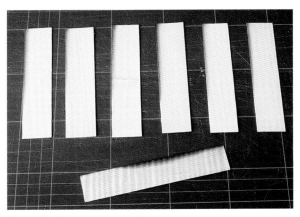

Figure 14: Spot the overcooked strip

the sand. The veneer should penetrate about ³/₄ of the depth of sand, without touching the pan base. Count six seconds, then remove the veneer. Check for shading. If no sign of shading exists, the sand is not up to temperature and a further period of heating is required. If the veneer appears charred black, or dark brown, then you have left the veneer in too long or the sand is already too hot. In this case, place a second veneer into the sand and count four seconds, then remove the veneer. It should now be somewhere near the required shading, about medium brown.

Practise with the remaining eight strips of veneer, checking that each one shades the same as the previous strips. Remember: subtlety and uniformity is what you are looking for. Cut and practise with more strips until you become proficient in the technique.

SHADING FOR FANS

An additional technique for producing shaded veneer strips for marquetry fans is necessary. To achieve this, use a scrap of veneer to pile the sand up across three-quarters of the pan surface, then flatten the sand to form a plateau. This should now leave about one-quarter of the pan surface completely clear of sand.

Using the sycamore or maple strips, place one strip edge-on into the plateau of sand so that about one-third of the veneer sticks out into the air. Leave for about four seconds and remove the

veneer. The resulting shading should appear as in Figure 14, with mid-brown uniform and light shading down one side, but the last third free of all shading. The unshaded portion is important because it creates a clear area in the centre of the fans. Spot the overcooked strip!

Any floral work will benefit from shading. The single white rose and the shell in chapter 2 require this technique, as do the flowers in the firescreen project in chapter 5.

Not every craftsperson uses this technique, however. Some rely on using different toned woods to achieve the same effect. It's a matter of taste and style how best you want to illustrate a shaded portion of art.

HAREWOOD

Harewood is a name used to describe treating wood with mineral substances to activate a chemical change, resulting in the colour of woods turning from their natural state to silver or grey. The origin of the word harewood is unknown, but the effect began appearing in furniture of the 17th and 18th centuries, when it was obtained by placing ferrous sulphate around the roots of a sycamore tree. This was performed about one or two years prior to felling and the result was that the wood turned a silver colour. We will look at other examples of treating trees to change the natural colour later in this chapter. Making harewood is Man's way of speeding up nature. The wood of certain trees, if given time, will change colour if the tree roots are exposed to certain mineral elements; iron compound traces in the soil can produce black or blue mineral staining in the wood. A hydrangea flower changes colour from pink to blue when the plants roots are exposed to a solution of ferrous sulphate, applied during the previous growing season.

Likewise, some veneers will change colour if immersed in the same solution. The difference is that, when immersed in the solution, a veneer will change colour within an hour or less, whereas a tree would take a full growing season for similar results to occur. Sycamore will only turn silver, whereas with other veneers the colour change varies from light to dark grey and in some cases to black. A selection of veneers that do make the harewood well are plane, sycamore, bird's-eye maple, crown maple, ash and beech.

Other veneers that have been treated successfully are: yew, masur birch, poplar, horse chestnut and aspen—and there will be many, many more which react to treatment. Harewoods are used for surface decoration on tabletops and cabinet-work. Silver or grey make an interesting contrast when set against natural, untreated timbers. In pictorial work, harewoods make realistic water effects—representing seas, lakes, streams and so on—as well as many landscape and building features.

As the natural tannin in veneers mixes with ferrous sulphates, a chemical reaction occurs through oxidization, causing a change from the veneer's natural state to a silver, grey or black colour. The best source for obtaining ferrous sulphate is your local garden centre.

The water used to dissolve the solution should be free of foreign elements which could nullify the chemical reaction necessary for making harewood. If your tapwater contains fluorides, calcium compounds or traces of ammonia, use distilled water, rainwater or melt ice from your freezer. Finally, a non-metallic container should be used as a 'bath' to immerse the veneers in the treated water. A decorator's plastic emulsion tray (unused) makes an ideal container, as illustrated in Figure 15.

Figure 15: Decorators plastic emulsion tray used as a bath

Sycamore is the veneer used commercially to produce silver harewood, but making your own and experimenting with other woods is not only cheaper but much more satisfying—and a bit of fun, too.

Sprinkle about 2 teaspoonfuls (20 gms) of ferrous sulphate into about 850 ml (1½ pints) of water, stir to dissolve the crystals, then fully immerse a veneer. Complete colour change occurs, in most cases, in an hour. Exceptionally, veneers have to be left longer to achieve results. Not all veneers react, though: in some cases the wood simply contains no tannin, which is necessary to kick-start the chemical change. It is advisable, when experimenting with a veneer you're not sure about, to check that the chemical change has affected the entire thickness of the veneer. Australian Silky Oak, for example, gives the impression that the chemical change has occurred, but sanding reveals that the change is only surface deep. Do not be caught out; if you are unsure if the treatment has worked, sand a small area of the veneer prior to using it. Commercially, harewood is made by immersing full leaves of sycamore, on edge, in an upright tub of solution and loosely coiling each leaf, allowing the chemical to work across the entire surface.

By accident, a colleague let some solution splash onto a sheet of untreated veneer when making harewood, and the following day he noticed a grey patch on his otherwise untouched sample. Realizing the possibilities this provided, he used the splashed area in a marquetry picture and it provided the artistic effect he was looking for. Trial (and error) paid off.

BLUE AND RED HAREWOOD

I am hugely indebted to my Italian marquetry friends for giving me samples of veneers which, at first glance, would appear to be dyed. Because of language translation difficulties at the time, I was not able to find out how these two woods had obtained the colour change you see in Figure 16, but I immediately recognized that both samples were beech (*fagaceae fagus*), or *fagio* as it is called in Italian. I could tell by the appearance that the samples could not have been dyed or treated after felling because the colour change was too irregular and natural-looking to be caused by any external chemical intervention.

The Techniques of Wood Surface Decoration, a book by David Hawkins, provides the explanation of the phenomenon: 'French cabinetmakers can make wood of any colour they please, by letting the roots of the trees absorb the coloured fluids the year before it is cut down. A solution of iron absorbed up one root, and of prussiate of potash up the other, will give the wood a permanent blue colour.' David Hawkins acknowledges a previous report on this topic in the *Scientific American* (vol. 3, no. 37, 3 June 1848, p. 296), which can be viewed on the magazine's website.

The other coloured beech in my example has streaks of green, yellow and orange with purple-to-red, and might have turned these colours by the tree absorbing, perhaps, red oxide up one root with copper sulphate up another (unless one of our readers knows different). These natural pigments and minerals would be absorbed into the sap of the tree, causing colour change to the heartwood over the annual growing cycle.

We are not suggesting that you dash into your garden armed with pots of pigment and natural mineral extracts and spread a mixture around your favourite fruit trees. However, marqueteurs and furniture makers would certainly welcome repeats of the beech examples shown in Figure 16, and it is an interesting question why more producers of veneers do not treat trees to produce these effects.

PENWORK

This is the technique of decorating marquetry work after the pattern is laid and pressed to the groundwork. The technique started to appear on English furniture in the late 18th century. Prior to that, the technique was used on Chinese artefacts to depict scenes with intricate detail. The combination of marquetry and penwork has a charm of its own. Personal items, such as boxes and portable writing desks, became very fashionable where first marquetry and then penwork was added, after applying one coat of polish.

Floral work, portraiture, costumes and animals depicted in marquetry all received this secondary process. Indian ink is applied onto the surface of the wood using a fine pointed lining pen. The fine lines are drawn on the veneer with the intention of giving detail to the design. The end result is very similar to the technique of sandshading, except that penwork highlights detail as well as shading. The two techniques also differ in that penwork is performed after the marquetry has been assembled and glued to the groundwork, whereas sandshading is carried out before or during assembly.

Penwork followed the more skilled technique of engraving, where a burin (a 'V'-shaped chisel)

Figure 16: Coloured beech

was used to gouge out a channel in the wood, which was then filled with a coloured pigment or dye. While penwork requires less skill than engraving, accuracy is important because the indelible ink does not give the artist a second chance. In general, the veneer used to illustrate the pattern or picture and receive the penwork is white in colour. The contrasting background veneer is usually very dark or black. Ebonized pear wood (pear dyed black to imitate ebony) is strongly evident on 18th- and 19th-century furniture. Typical examples are to be found in the Museobottega in Sorrento, Italy.

English cabinetmakers of the same period used the technique to decorate their work. The matching pier tables made by Chippendale are a good example, where the central half-round fans are finely decorated. Today, there is a strong school of thought that penwork distracts from the true skill of marquetry, and certainly where hobbyists are concerned, fine lines, dots for eyes and other minute details are skilfully achieved by

inserting slivers of wood. This technique is discussed below.

Despite opinions for and against the technique, penwork is still evident today on Italian furniture, where tables, trays and musical boxes are produced for export across the world.

FINE LINES

In general, the need for inserting fine lines to a marquetry design occurs more in pictorial marquetry than in furniture. Typical needs are to depict a ship's rigging, whiskers on animals and strands of hair. The lines are inserted during construction.

Examples of fine lines appear on the firescreen shown in the Gallery in chapter 6. The antennae of the butterflies were inserted prior to gluing and mounting, using fine lines of black sycamore.

As an experiment some years ago, I produced a picture of our dog Kelly. A Cairn terrier typical of her breed, she is scruffy haired but appealing (Figure 17), and therefore I wanted to capture

1 Place a steel rule along the edge of a short piece of black-'dyed sycamore, making sure the rule is in line with the direction of the grain of the wood. Position the rule so that only about 1 mm is protruding from under the rule. With the scalpel held vertically, cut off the protruding 1 mm of veneer. Without moving the rule, angle the scalpel into the veneer at about 5° to the vertical, as shown above. You should cut off the thinnest of slivers, causing the sliver to curl as you cut it away.

2 Cut a fine groove into a background veneer. Then, cut to one side of the groove by the thinnest margin to remove slivers less than 0.25 mm wide. Starting at one end of the opened groove and holding the cut black sliver in your hand, insert one end using the back of the scalpel. Once in place, put a spot of PVA glue onto the end to secure it.

Figure 17 Use of fine lines in pictorial marquetry

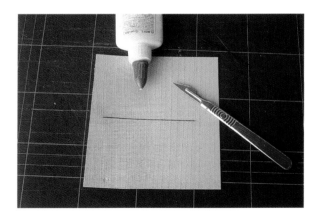

3 The curled sliver can be slowly eased into the cut groove. The curl of the sliver helps the insertion. Use the back of the scalpel blade to tease the sliver into place. Finally, as the sliver reaches the end of the groove, cut the sliver trim with the end and rub PVA glue into the completed line. If you turn the veneer over you should see the sliver appearing at the back, proving that it is inserted through to the full thickness of veneer.

the unruly state of her hair. I could have used a figured veneer in sheet form to depict the hair, but, as an experiment, I chose to use fine lines instead. Initially, I used normal whole veneers for the ears, nose, eyes and mouth. For the hair, literally hundreds of fine lines were cut from a range of different coloured veneers. I cut out small areas at a time from the dyed blue bird's-eye maple background veneer, and after pouring a pool of PVA glue into the window (using masking tape to prevent it escaping), I spread bundles of fine lines into the glue. After placing paper and boards either side and pressing it, I added more glue and fine lines until the window was proud of the background. Continuing in this fashion across the picture, I was able to build up the hair and be selective where I wanted a particular colour. On completion I simply sanded the fine lines flat to the background and enjoyed the result. Kelly has gained much admiration at craft shows, particularly from artists, and of course animal lovers. The message here is never be afraid to experiment. Wood-surface decoration has experienced many techniques over the last four centuries. Some, like sandshading and penwork, have survived, while others, like engraving, have disappeared completely from the repertoire of marquetry techniques. It's up to future generations first to experience the past, then experiment, develop and excite the world of woodcraft with their own brand of bold and imaginative ideas.

There's a quotation by an unknown author, which reads:

Do not follow where the path may lead
Go instead where there is no path
and leave a trail!

As you begin chapter 2 and examine and build the patterns created by those 18th century English masters of neo-classical design, you will quickly realize that, by example, they collectively blazed a trail that designers and furniture makers across the world have followed for the last two-hundred-and-fifty years.

CHAPTER TWO

TUTORIALS

HISTORICAL BACKGROUND

'Inlay motifs', as most of the standard 18th-century marquetry patterns have come to be known, were first introduced as plaster casts for decorating ceilings and cornices. Robert Adam (1728–92), the renowned Scottish architect and designer, is recognized for making fans, shells and paterae (singular: patera) fashionable additions to the design of interior doors in many stately homes around Britain.

In 1767, Thomas Chippendale (1718–79), the most famous of all English furniture makers, worked with Adam at Harewood House, near Leeds in Yorkshire. Edwin Lascelles, then owner of the newly built house, gave Chippendale the greatest commission of his career—to furnish the house from top to bottom. Chippendale and Adam saw the opportunity to collaborate and produce designs that would create a specific style (now called the neo-classical) embracing both plasterwork and furniture. The result is that today, corner fans, oval fans and semi-circular fans, as well as shells, urns, swags, anthemions and floral work are as strongly evident in Chippendale

Figure 1: Diana and Minerva commode, Harewood House

furniture as they are in Adam's outstanding ceilings and cornices.

Other renowned cabinetmakers of that and later periods, such as Sheraton and Hepplewhite, also used these designs (disseminated in publications such as Chippendale's book, *The Gentleman and Cabinet Maker's Director*, 1754). Their continuing popularity 250 years later speaks for itself.

One feature most inlay motifs have in common is that they depend heavily on sandshading, a technique of scorching veneers in hot silver sand to achieve an impressive three-dimensional effect (see the *Sandshading* section in chapter 1 for details). This, and the fact that some fan designs can be constructed from templates, makes them the perfect motif for introducing students to two of the craft's basic techniques.

Marquetry fans remind me of my first working days as an apprentice organ tuner and renovator. The shape of the fans bears a close resemblance to the organ pipes that decorate church interiors, for instance at my local Town Hall in Leeds. Above the majestic organ frontage, which dominates the Victoria Hall, sits a giant forty-flute circular fan measuring some 6 m (20 ft) or more in diameter. Perhaps the work by architect Cuthbert Broderick in the 19th century indicates that he believed, like me, that the affinity between Adam's fans and the décor of organs was too strong to ignore. We know that Adam worked on projects with John Snetzer, a renowned Swiss organ-builder. Was it this association, perhaps, that offered Adam an opportunity to illustrate his musical passions using his artistic skills?

With the history that these motifs embody in our minds, let us begin the first tutorial and hope that you, like many others, will continue to build and enjoy these timeless creations.

ASSEMBLING FANS BY THE TEMPLATE METHOD

Templates begin life as paper designs that need to be transferred onto wooden boards. Medium Density Fibreboard (MDF) makes the ideal medium for this purpose. Once a template is built, it can be stored in the workshop and re-used over and over again, in the knowledge that future constructions will be identical in size and shape to earlier productions.

Marquetry fans are found on items of furniture and fittings around homes throughout Europe, appearing on table legs, table tops, carver chair backs, cabinet tops, cabinet doors and drawers, trays, jewellery boxes, wood-surround fireplaces, mirror frames and so on. Of all the motifs made in marquetry, the fan occurs more than any other. Generally, fans appear as corner fans, oval fans, circular fans, half-round fans and diamond fans, each type changing size and shape depending on its application. Similarly, the number of flutes that make up a fan changes with size and design requirements, ranging from a four-flute corner fan found on cabinet doors and drawer fronts to the impressive 28-fluted oval fan found sometimes on cabinets and the centrepieces of gallery trays.

The first two tutorials teach you how to make three types of fan. Both the outward- and inward-curving corner fan are illustrated, followed by the 28-fluted oval fan. Once you have followed the technique for constructing these, other shaped fans can be made in exactly the same way. It is only a matter of transferring the paper design onto an MDF board and following the tutorials given here.

Each of the paper designs can be found in the Appendix. You may have to scale the dimensions up or down to suit the application you are working on but the standard design pattern will remain the same.

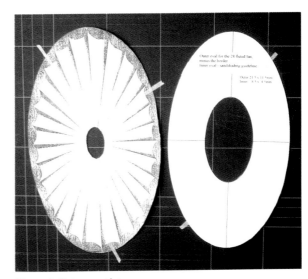

Figure 2: Paper templates

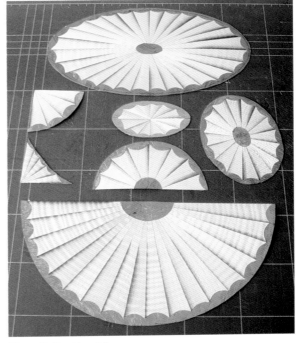

Figure 3: Samples of fans

TUTORIAL No. 1: CONVEX CORNER FAN

TOOLS REQUIRED

Scalpel

Steel rule

Compass

Protractor

Pencil

Silver sand, hot stove and pan

Cutting board

Cutting mat

MATERIALS REQUIRED

6 mm (¼ in) MDF board, 150 mm (6 in) square

Sycamore or maple veneer, 130 mm (5 in) square

Any redwood or burr veneer, 100 mm (4 in) square

Veneer tape

Masking tape

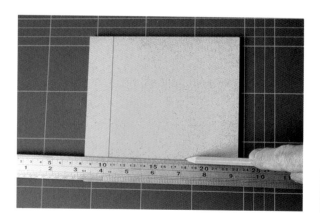

1 Using a steel rule, draw two pencil lines, a ruler width from two adjacent edges of the MDF board. Place a pencil into your compass and set the radius to 50 mm (2 in).

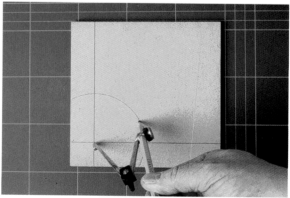

2 Draw two arcs, one at 50 mm and a smaller arc at a radius of 15 mm (⅝ in), with the compass point held where the two border lines intersect. Extend the larger arc into the two border areas, as shown.

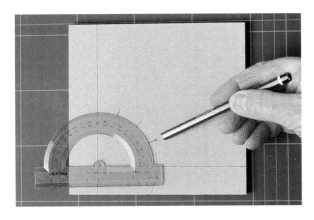

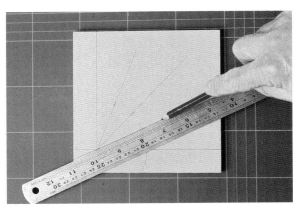

3 Line up your protractor so that the 0° and 90° marks correspond with the two border lines. Make three pencil marks, one at 45° and two that bisect on either side, namely 22.5° and 67.5°. Naturally it is not possible to be ultra-precise to half a degree, but be as close as is humanly possible.

4 Using your steel rule, line up each mark with the axis of the two borders. Extend the lines into the outer edges of the MDF board, as shown.

That completes the template design. Now you are ready to prepare the veneers.

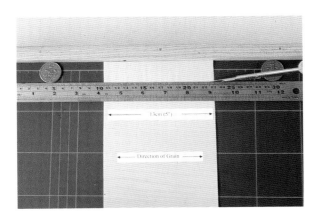

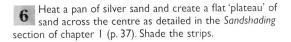

5 Cut 4 strips of sycamore (or maple) veneer, each 130 mm (5 in) long and 25 mm (1 in) wide, with the grain running along the length of each strip. Use your marquetry cutting board and two 2p coins as spacers. (A 2p coin happens to measure 25 mm in diameter.)

6 Heat a pan of silver sand and create a flat 'plateau' of sand across the centre as detailed in the *Sandshading* section of chapter 1 (p. 37). Shade the strips.

7 Place the first veneer strip as shown. Make sure the shaded area of the veneer lies between the two arcs. The area below the small arc (shown in red) should be free of shading. This is important for the final finished appearance. Hold this veneer in place with masking tape. Position your steel rule across the first flute line and cut through the veneer. This completes the first flute.

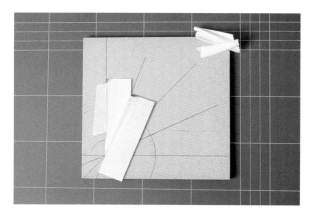

8 Place the second strip with the shaded side joined edge-to-edge against the first strip. Again check that the shaded area ends at the small arc. This time secure the two strips together with veneer tape. Lick the tape, making it very wet. Place across the joint and rub dry. As the tape dries, it contracts and tightens the joint. Make sure the tape covers the area over the large arc. You can overlap veneer tape without any problems.

9 After fitting and cutting the four flutes, make sure the assembly is held to the MDF board with a few tabs of masking tape.
   Scribe a second arc with your compass, set to a radius of 50 mm (2 in), as shown above.

10 Use a 2p coin to form the scallops at the end of each flute. Push the coin into the flute until you can see where the coin meets the two sides of the flute and the arc that you drew with your compass. Draw round the coin. Do this for all four flutes.

11 Using your scalpel, cut through each curved scallop, but make sure veneer tape exists where you're going to cut. The fragile points at the ends of each flute will certainly break unless protected with tape. Cut through each scallop in turn. Make a light cut first, then go over the same cuts again, this time pressing harder until you cut through. The practice exercises in the *Using the Knife* section of chapter 1 (p. 28) help beginners to understand the technique of free-hand cutting.

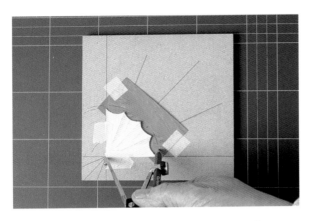

12 Take a small piece of decorative border veneer (burrs are ideal) about 80 x 50 mm (3 x 2 in) in size. With the grain running along the length of the veneer (note: burr veneers consist of end-grain, so the direction of grain does not apply) place the piece under the four flutes, and secure to the board with masking tape. Set your compass to a radius of 55 mm (2¼ in) (5 mm/¹⁄₄ in larger than the first arc) and scribe an arc across the border veneer as shown.

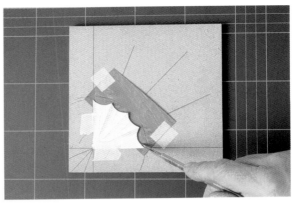

13 Score a line with your scalpel where the 4 scallops meet the border veneer. Place the scalpel at an angle of about 2° from the vertical (no more) and score a line across the border veneer. Start at a flute nearest your body and move forwards step-by-step, scoring into the veneer. Make upright stab marks where the points of the flutes are. Score all the 4 scallops and remove the border veneer.

14 With your scalpel held vertical to the veneer, cut squarely through the scored line until the waste is removed. Cut through the pencil line that forms the arc. Offer the cut border to the 4 fluted scallops and check for a tight fit. Secure the 2 together with veneer tape. Finally, cut away the overhanging side pieces on either side of the border veneer. The corner fan is now complete.

Turn the fan over and admire your work.

Note that the veneer tape must stay on until the fan is glued to its intended application.

The tape is easily removed simply by wetting, which causes the tape to swell so that it can be pushed off the veneers using the end of a steel rule.

TUTORIAL NO. 2: FIVE-FLUTE CONCAVE CORNER FAN

The fans shown above consist of six flutes and are mounted into the surround without a border. This tutorial shows how to make a five-fluted inward-curving fan, but you can substitute the six-fluted version, while still following the same instructions.

TOOLS REQUIRED

Scalpel

Steel rule

Pencil

2p or 5p coin (or other coins of 25mm [1 in] and 18mm [¾ in] diameter respectively)

Silver sand, hot stove and pan

Cutting board

Cutting mat

MATERIALS REQUIRED

6 mm (¼ in) MDF board, 150 mm (6 in) square

Sycamore or maple veneer, 130 mm (5 in) square

Any redwood veneer (burr of mahogany, sepele, etc.), 100 mm (4 in) square

Veneer tape

Masking tape

Sharpening stone, to regrind point on scalpel blade

1 Copy the template given in the Appendix and carefully cut out the paper design using a scalpel. Using a piece of MDF about 155mm (6 in) square, draw two datum lines, a ruler width from the edge down two adjacent sides. Tape the paper design as shown and mark off the 4 lines of the flutes. Also draw around the curve of the fan using the paper pattern as a template. Retain the paper design for later use.

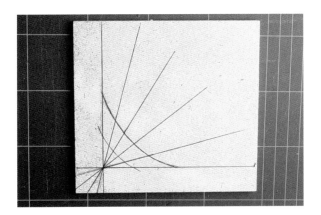

2 Line up the rule with the marks of the four flutes and the central axis, and extend the lines as shown. Draw a smaller arc (freehand) that starts and finishes 25mm (1 in) from the 90° axis. The arc is shown in red for clarity. You're now ready to build the fan.

3 Cut and sandshade five strips of sycamore by following steps five and six of the previous tutorial (convex corner fan, p.45). Tape the first flute with masking tape to the left-hand side of the template. Line a steel rule along the first co-ordinate and cut through the veneer with a scalpel. Fit the second flute up to the first making sure the sandshaded area stops at the inner arc (red line). Secure the two veneers together with veneer tape.

4 Complete all five flutes. Lay the paper template back across the flutes and draw around the curve of the template using the edge of the paper as a guide. Make two marks (shown as red arrows) about 3 mm (1/8 in) inside the ends of the paper template. Remove the template.

5 Use a coin of 25mm (1 in) or 18mm (3/4 in) diameter to draw the scallops around the ends of each flute.

6 Place the fan onto your cutting mat and cut around the curves using the scalpel. It is important that veneer tape is positioned where you are cutting the scallops. The tiny points will break if not protected with tape.

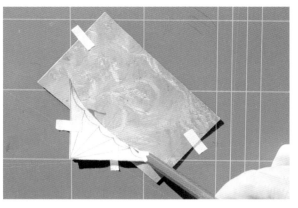

7 Lay the paper template across the red veneer (burr is best) and draw around the curve with a pencil.

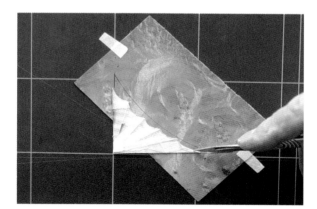

8 Lay the fan up to the curved line and centre it so that an equal border shows across the ends of the fan. Secure both assemblies and score around the flutes with a scalpel. Remove the fan and cut through the scored line and through the pencilled curve.

9 Marry the border to the fan and secure together with veneer tape. That completes the fan assembly.

TUTORIAL NO. 3: 28-FLUTE OVAL FAN

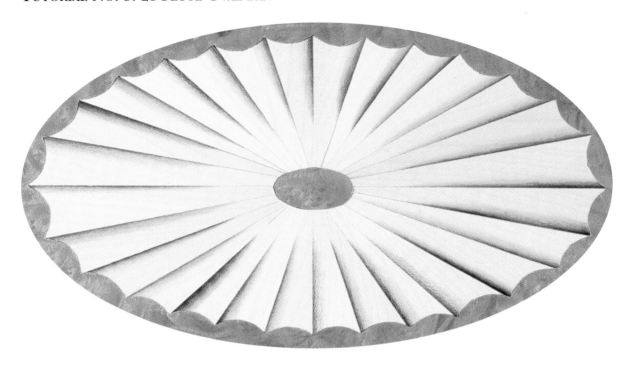

TOOLS REQUIRED

Scalpel
Steel rule
Pencil
2 x 2p coins (or other coins of 25 mm / 1 in diameter)
Silver sand, hot stove and pan
Long-nosed tweezers
Cutting board
Cutting mat

1 Cut a piece of MDF or ply about 250 mm (10 in) wide and 150 mm (6 in) high. Draw *x* and *y* co-ordinates centrally across the board as shown.

Make two photocopies of the template (p. 162). Cut out the largest and smallest oval on one copy, for use at step 2. Cut out the second-largest and second-smallest ovals on the other copy, for use at steps 4 and 14. You may find it helpful to make hardboard or plywood templates from the paper originals.

MATERIALS REQUIRED

6 mm (¼ in) MDF board, 250 x 150 mm (10 x 6 in)
Veneer tape
Masking tape
Redwood veneer, 250 x 150 mm (10 x 6 in), grain along long axis
Sycamore veneer, 700 x 130 mm (28 x 5 in), grain along short axis

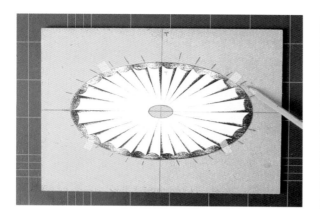

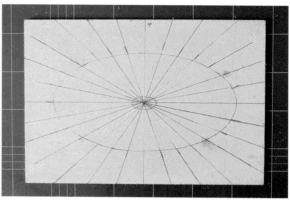

2 Line up the large paper template with the *xy* co-ordinates and secure in place with 4 tabs of masking tape. Draw around the inner and outer ovals with a pencil, thus transferring both shapes to the MDF. Register the top of the template and the MDF board with the letter 'T'. Extend the 28 flutes by marking with pencil as illustrated.

3 Line up the steel rule across each opposing diagonal and draw pencil lines through the design, extending the lines about 5 cm (2 in) beyond the template. Complete this for each of the 28 flutes. Retain the paper template.

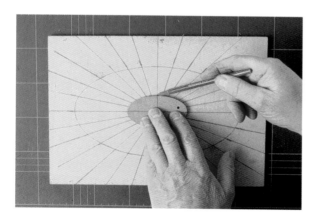

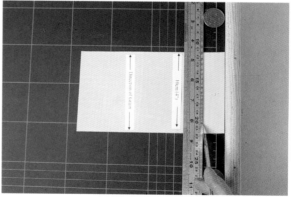

4 Using the smallest template, line it up with the *xy* co-ordinates and draw a pencil line around the inner oval (we used a wood template here). This oval line will become a guide for laying the sandshaded strips of veneers, as will be evident later. Remove the template.

5 Prepare some sycamore or maple veneer for making 14 strips 130 mm (5 in) long and 14 strips 100 mm (4 in) long. Use two 2p coins as spacers and on your marquetry cutting board cut the strips as shown. Cut a few spares of each size in case some are not sandshaded correctly. *Note the direction of grain.*

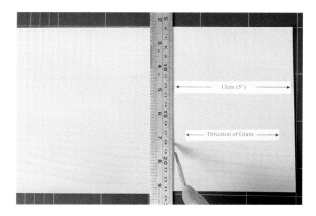

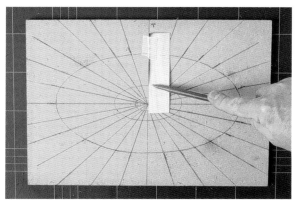

6 The 130 mm (5 in) veneer strips are for the flutes at the two ends of the oval, while the 100 mm (4 in) strips are for the flutes along the two middle areas. Sandshade each of the veneer strips along one of the sides. Follow the instructions given in the *Sandshading* section of chapter 1 (p. 37). Make sure you achieve an even shading across all strips and leave one-third of the length unshaded, as detailed in chapter 1.

7 Lay the first strip of veneer with the sandshaded side in line with the top flute at 12 o'clock on the design. Make sure the sandshaded area of the veneer lies in the area between the outer and middle ovals. Hence the need for that oval shown in red. The area below the red oval must be clear of shading. Make sure the veneer covers some of the centre oval space.

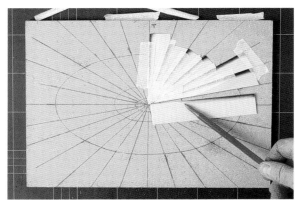

8 Hold this first strip (only) to the MDF board with masking tape. Place a rule across the first co-ordinates at 1 o'clock (or 11 o'clock if left-handed). Using a light sweeping cut first, cut along the side of the rule with the scalpel, getting firmer with each cut, until the veneer waste is removed. That's the first of 28 flutes inserted.

9 Place each strip edge-to-edge against the previous strip, moving clockwise around the design (anti-clockwise if left-handed). Make three checks on each strip:

1. The strip must overlap the outer oval.
2. The sandshading must end at the middle (red) oval.
3. The strip must overlap part of the centre oval.

Note that the veneer tape must stay on until the fan is glued to its intended application (see p. 47).

After laying the first strip, all the remaining strips will be held together using veneer tape. It's very important to lick this tape well, making it very wet. Place the wet tape over the joint of the two veneers and rub the tape with your fingers until it dries. As it dries, the tape contracts and tightens the joint being held. You must also make sure the tape covers the area around the outer curve. You can overlap this tape if needed.

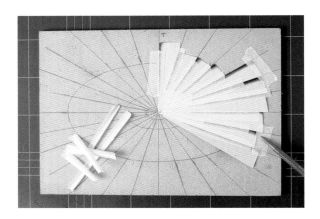

10 As the pattern builds up on the template, place tabs of masking tape every 5 or 6 strips to the outer edges of the veneers. This prevents the assembly slipping off line.

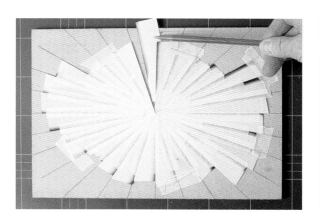

11 To lay the final, 28th flute, first remove the masking tape from the first flute. Slide the final strip under the edge of the first flute and bring it up to the edge of the 27th flute. Check the sandshaded area is correct and that the strip reaches into the centre oval. Secure the strip to the 27th flute with veneer tape.

12 Place the steel rule across the top of the first strip, bringing it in line with the shaded edge. Using the scalpel, cut through the 28th flute, making sure you reach into the centre of the design to cut away all the surplus veneer.

13 Turn the first two or three flutes back and remove the surplus veneer from the 28th flute. Secure the last and first flutes together with veneer tape. Finally, write a letter 'T' on the tape of the 28th flute, so that you can identify the top of the assembly.

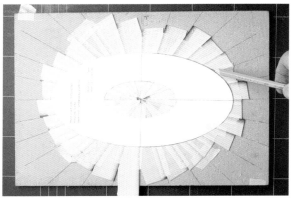

14 Place the second-largest paper template, lining it up carefully with the *xy* co-ordinates across the flutes. Hold with tabs of tape, then draw a pencil line around the outer oval by resting the pencil against the edge of the paper template. Remove the paper template.

15 Place a 2p coin (or another coin of 25 mm / 1 in diameter) so that it just touches the two joints of a flute on each side of the coin. Draw around the coin with a pencil. Repeat this for each flute. This creates the scallops at the ends of each flute. Ensure that veneer tape is in place where you are drawing the scallops. Remove the assembled fan from the MDF board after drawing all 28 scallops.

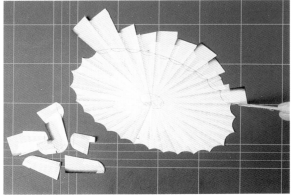

16 Place the assembly onto the cutting mat. Using a scalpel, start at a scallop nearest your body and make a vertical stab cut at the start of one scallop. Move the knife forwards about 6 mm (¹/₄ in) and cut through the pencil line and veneer by pulling the knife towards the first stab cut. Continue these steps until you reach the end of the scallop. Turn the fan assembly over to see the finished effect. Although this is the back of the fan (the side to be glued down), it gives you an idea how the face side will look after assembly and tape removal.

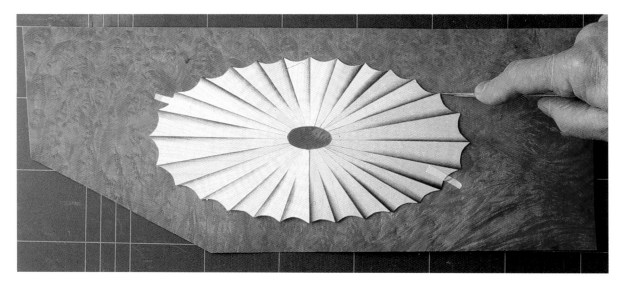

You should now see why it's important to have veneer tape where you cut the scallops. Without the tape, the two points forming the scallop would break because of the short grain.

17 Cut all the scallops in the same way. For the border you need the largest paper template and a sheet of decorative veneer (colour of your choice), approximately 250 x 150 mm (10 x 6 in). Burr woods make excellent borders for fans. Tape the fan across the veneer and score around the 28 scallops. Remove the fan and cut out the scored lines. Remove the window and insert the fan.

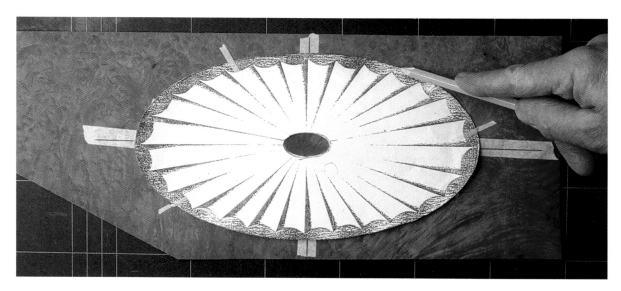

18 Place veneer tape in line with the *xy* co-ordinates, then line up the largest template. Draw around the template with pencil to create the oval shape. Cut around the pencil line.

Finally, turn the fan over and examine your efforts. You should be looking for even sandshading, a clean centre without shading, and a border of equal width.

The tape should stay on until the fan has been glued and mounted to your chosen furniture item. After the glue has dried, wet the tape and push it off with the end of the steel rule.

THE WINDOW METHOD

The window method of construction offers marqueteurs the scope to express themselves more artistically than any other type of construction. Introduced some fifty years ago by the Marquetry Society of Great Britain, the method has become the accepted technique among hobbyists for making pictures and decorating small items of furniture.

In its simplest form, the window method consists of cutting out a shape from one veneer, which is called the window, and filling the hole with another veneer of the same shape, which is called the insert. The insert veneer is carefully selected and positioned in the window so that the grain, figure, texture and colour give an artistic representation of the object under construction.

From its advent, the window method allowed marqueteurs to go to amazing lengths to achieve remarkable realism in their work. Inserting a veneer into a window can now range from one large veneer—to represent a sky, a distant mountain or the wall of a building, say—to the thinnest sliver to represent a cat's whisker or the pupil of an eye. Portraiture has become commonplace, while birds, butterflies and tigers can look like they will leap out of the very wood they are made from.

For centuries, floral work included in furniture decoration has been built with a fretsaw. While the tool is still a very important part of the craft and its use and effect is amply detailed in this book (see chapter 1, p. 35), it cannot compete with the window method when 'realism' is what is required.

Two floral designs are included in the following tutorials. The first, a compass rose, is standard for furniture application and consists of straight-line cutting. A compass rose offers beginners an opportunity to produce an appealing design that takes on a three-dimensional effect when the construction is completed. It also allows you to experiment with variations in the design, prompting fresh ideas along the way, we hope.

The second tutorial calls for individual expression. The single rose—with its leaves, stem and sharpest of thorns—makes a good subject for the lid of the jewellery box project given in chapter 5. A single rose inset across the lid of the box can transform this project into a romantic mission!

The compass rose is perhaps the oldest design in this book. Dating back to the 16th century when early compasses consisted of just 4 pointers—north, south, east and west—which eventually advanced to 6 pointers, then 8, then 12 points, which represents the 5-minute intervals of a clock face. Finally, the 16-pointed rose became the modern standard, consisting of 8 large points, each separated by 8 smaller points. The design given here has many applications. With its 16 points radiating outwards like a modern sunburst, the design looks impressive set either as a centrepiece for an occasional table, a tray or a box lid. By selecting two contrasting veneers, the compass points take on a three-dimensional appearance.

Figure 1: Compass rose

TUTORIAL NO. 4: COMPASS ROSE

TOOLS REQUIRED

Scalpel

Steel rule

Line drawing design

Cutting mat and board

2 x 5p coins (or other coins of 18 mm / ³⁄₄ in diameter)

Compass and protractor (only needed if the sizes are to be changed
  from the design provided)

MATERIALS REQUIRED

Dyed black and maple harewood used here (red and white veneers
  could be used instead), 300 mm (12 in) lengths

Any contrasting background veneer (Burr ash used here)

Veneer tape

Masking tape

Paper glue

A completed design drawing is given in the Appendix, p. 163. If you wish to change the dimensions from those given, all that is needed is to change the radii of the four circles, but at the same time maintaining their ratios. A compass and protractor will be required to redraw the design, but the method of construction follows the step-by-step procedures given below. The first step is to pre-assemble the two veneers, representing the compass points.

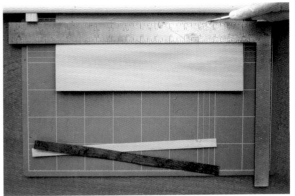

1 Using the design given in the Appendix, first make a photocopy, then cut out the paper pattern by cutting about 12 mm (1/2 in) beyond the outer circle. Using any suitable paper gum, stick the paper template onto the selected background veneer and press flat by hand.

2 Using your cutting mat and two suitable spacers such as 2p or 5p coins, cut six strips of veneer about 300 mm (12 in) long. Cut three of the strips from dyed black sycamore and the other three of silver harewood (treated sycamore), or two veneers of your own choice. The width of each strip must be about 6 mm (1/4 in) wider than half the widest part of one large compass point. The grain must run down the length of each strip.

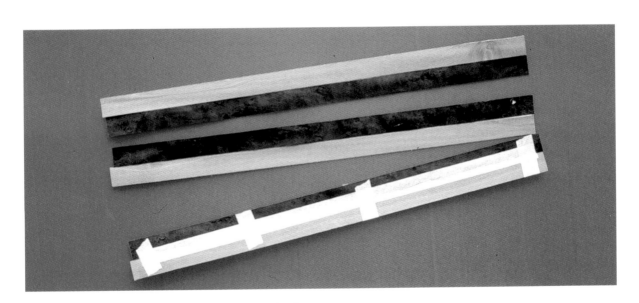

3 Place one silver strip alongside one black strip and make sure it's a tight edge-to-edge joint. Secure the joint with veneer tape along its length. Do this by first sticking small tabs of tape across the two veneers, then stick one long length between the two end tabs. Overlap the tapes slightly. Repeat with the other strips.

4 We are now ready to cut out the first of the eight large compass points, shown in red. Using a steel rule and scalpel, lay the rule alongside one of the four lines, which form a large compass point. Make a stab cut at the point nearest you. Keep the blade up against the rule and draw the knife down the veneer towards you until it engages the stab mark. One or more strokes might be needed to cut through the paper and veneer. Move the workpiece around and repeat this operation to cut through the other three sides of the compass point. Try to cut the points as sharp as possible.

5 Turn the assembly over so you are looking at the back. Place one of the pre-assembled strips under the window with the taped side facing away from you. Align the strip so that the centre joint of the two veneers exactly lines up with the top and bottom points of the window. Tape the insert strip to the main assembly securely, using masking tape. You will begin to see the wisdom of pre-assembling the two veneers. Having them held together makes alignment with the compass points much easier.

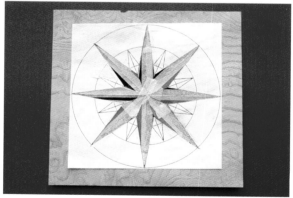

6 Using your scalpel, score around the joint where the insert veneer meets the main veneer. After scoring, put the strip onto your cutting mat and, following the scored line, cut out the compass point. Insert the compass point into the window from the back and run a thin bead of PVA around the joint. Rub the glue into the joint until it dries.

7 Repeat for the remaining large points, making sure the colours alternate, black/silver/black etc. from one point to another. The face side of the assembly should look like this.

8 Cut out all eight small compass points, following the lines of the drawing on the face side. When you have finished, turn the assembly over; it should look like this (note that the red background is only to highlight the illustration—you should be using a cutting mat).

9 Insert each of the eight points in turn, making sure the black/silver colours are laid on opposite sides to the large points. This way the colours alternate black/silver all round the design.

10 The face side should have the tape and the paper design still on the veneers. Leave them on until you have glued and press the assembly to its intended application. To remove the papers, wet them to cause them to swell, then use the end of a steel rule to push them off, or use a cabinet scraper.

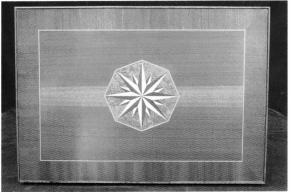

11 This construction leaves the design cut directly into a background veneer. An additional step would be to join up the eight 'flats' across the tips of the large compass points, using 1.5 mm ($^1/_{16}$ in) stringing, as illustrated here (see the *stringing and banding* section in chapter 3).

TUTORIAL NO. 5: A SINGLE ROSE

TOOLS REQUIRED

Scalpel
Pencil
Silver sand, hot stove and pan
Line drawing

MATERIALS REQUIRED

Poplar veneer, 150 mm (6 in) square
Sycamore veneer, 100 mm (4 in) square
Indian rosewood or other dark brown veneer, 100 mm (4 in) square
Sepele or kevesinga veneer, 100 mm (4 in) square
Any veneer to use as waster, 150 mm (6 in) square
Carbon paper
Masking tape
PVA glue

The veneer selection given above is to make a white rose, but other colours can be made using the following veneers: ash burr—off-white; madrona burr—pink; pear—pinky-purple; cherry—pale pink; obeche—creamy-white; Rosa peroba—rose-red. A line drawing of the rose is given in the Appendix, p. 161.

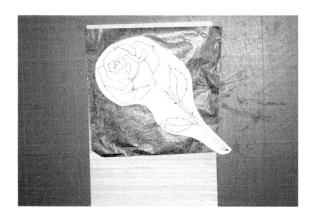

1 Position the line drawing over a waster veneer and tape in place across the top edge. Place the sheet of carbon paper under the drawing with the carbon side facing the waster veneer. Using a pencil, or an empty ballpoint pen (without ink), carefully draw around the line to transfer the drawing to the waster. A waster veneer is preferred to the actual veneer the rose will be cut into. This way the finished rose can be positioned precisely where it looks best.

2 To build the white rose, you need two veneers: poplar (left) and sycamore. It's best to sandshade the four edges of the sheet of poplar before building up the rose. This allows you to select which part of the veneer you want to use for each petal. The sycamore veneer will be used to represent the top edges of those petals which curl over. Don't sandshade the sycamore.

3 Start assembly from the bottom of the drawing and work upwards to prevent getting carbon on your hands. Make step cuts as described in the knife cutting exercises in chapter 1 (p. 30).

4 Start at one of the outer areas and cut out one petal. Slide the poplar veneer behind the window and turn it until a small amount of shading is shown on the base of the petal. This gives the petal 'depth of field'—a three-dimentional feel—and creates a curving image. Note that the petals to the left and right of the bottom petal are cut in before cutting in the curled edge of the bottom petal. This requires you to realign the paper drawing exactly, and redraw the curled edge using the carbon paper.

5 The inner petals are best depicted with lighter-coloured top edges, and this is where the sycamore comes in. First, cut in the lower part of the petal, making sure to use some area of sandshading to provide depth of field to the petal. Secondly, cut out the curled-over top part of the petal and slide the sycamore behind the window. Turn it around until the grain is running parallel across the width of the petal. Cut it out and insert in the normal way.

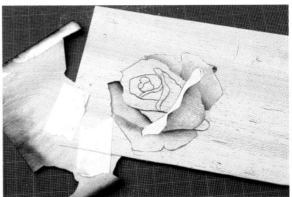

6 Insert the curled edge, represented by the sycamore veneer, and glue in with PVA. Already the rose is taking on some realism. Note that, unlike in the previous tutorials, veneer tape is not needed to hold the pieces together. The smallest beads of PVA rubbed into the joints leave the rose visible throughout construction. This lets you judge the artistic effect as you progress.

7 As you proceed towards the centre of the rose, you need to insert a few darker areas to create depth. Also, the curled part of the petals get thinner as you near the centre. Working to the line drawing and getting the sandshading in the right place is the secret of building a realistic rose.

8 This piece surrounds the centre of the rose and needs sandshading on the inside of the curve. You will notice that the insert (right of assembly) is not sandshaded at this stage. Step 9 explains how to achieve shading to the inside of this awkwardly shaped piece.

9 Place the end of an old teaspoon into the jaws of a metalworking vice and squeeze the tip of the spoon together to form a channel. This allows you to direct hot sand exactly where you want it. Hold the piece with the tweezers and pour the sand so that it falls onto the area in question, where it will start to scorch. You can see in the picture that the outside of the piece is free from shading. The spoon is a simple but very effective tool.

10 The finished rose can be removed from its waster and used to decorate the lid of a jewellery box. In this way, you can position the rose across a chosen background veneer to give the best impact.

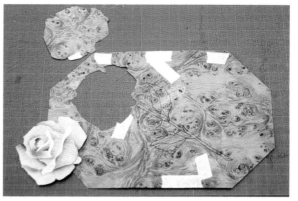

11 Hold the rose in place with tabs of masking tape while you 'back-cut' it into the veneer. This means using the rose as a template to score around the petals. After scoring, cut the background veneer out on your cutting mat to create the window for the rose. Insert the rose from the back. Glue in place with a few drops of PVA.

12 Cut out the stalk of the rose, including the two thorns. Select a dark brown veneer, such as Indian rosewood (very appropriate for this project). It will stand out from the background. Cut it into the window in the normal manner. Place some veneer tape across the rosewood to prevent it breaking up while cutting.

13 Cut in the leaves, half a leaf at a time. In the example here, green Cyprus burr veneer was used (a timber that's sadly no longer available). You could use green magnolia as an alternative, or a red veneer. It may surprise you to know that on many roses the leaves nearest the flower turn red. Check it out!

The finished white rose is used to decorate the jewellery box project detailed in chapter 5.

THE FRETSAW METHOD

The fretsaw is the oldest method of cutting veneers, and is still in existence today. It dates back to the early part of the 16th century, when veneers were sawn off the log in thicknesses of about 2 mm ($^1/_8$ in). In fact, some exotic veneers are still sawn-cut but the majority are sliced from the log by means of a guillotine. Today, veneers are cut into shapes using a fretsaw (called a coping saw in the US) where the vertical action of the blade performs the cut. This was not the case until the latter part of the 18th century when a bench-mounted saw called a 'donkey' was invented to saw through veneers with the blade held horizontal to the work—the reason being that, without the benefit of electricity, craftsmen had to rely on natural daylight to perform close-cutting work such as this. It consisted of a bench that the craftsman mounted—as if straddling a donkey—raising him off the floor. The saw was positioned at the very top of the wooden frame, thereby elevating the work high enough to allow the frame and the man to be positioned under a window, thereby gaining maximum daylight.

Despite the difficult working conditions, furniture makers from the 16th to the 18th centuries produced work of remarkable quality. Their exquisitely crafted marquetry and parquetry decorations are now proudly preserved in stately homes and museums across Europe.

It is also encouraging that fretsawn marquetry is still widely practised across Europe and North America to this day. Hand-held and motorized fretsaws, ultra-thin blades, and thinly cut veneers provide the basis on which small- to medium-sized workshops thrive in a highly competitive craft-orientated industry. Chapter 1 details today's fretsawing tools and equipment.

The following tutorials detail the three-stage techniques (building the 'pad', fretsawing, and assembling the design) which, despite the intro-duction of modern tools and equip-ment, have witnessed little change from those early days. These techniques will no doubt continue for as long as customers across the world demand wood-surface decoration of their furniture. The three techniques accompany two 18th-century designs—the shell and patera—which provide the perfect subjects to get you started. These have been chosen for a number of reasons: they are achievable for beginners; they allow furniture restorers to effect repairs to two popular decorations; and they require the all-important sandshading to provide the necessary artistic realism.

Figure 1: Fretwork, by student Alan Rollinson, York College

TUTORIAL NO. 6: SHELL

The shell is an ideal design to get you started with the fretsaw. First, because it is relatively small and consists of only a few pieces, and second, because the design appears on tens of thousands of pieces of antique furniture across the world. If you are working or intend to work in furniture restoration, you will certainly be required to repair or replace this design at some time in your working life. Like many motifs they suffer damage from either water spillage or the effects of central heating in modern homes. Figure 2 shows some of the different shell designs you could encounter. There are others as well, and you may need to search through catalogues and reference books to find the one you want.

The horn-styled shell was introduced during the late 18th century, on small furniture items such as clocks, trays, sewing boxes and personalized boxes. Because of the variation in styles, furniture restorers have the ongoing problem of matching the right style of shell to the damaged original, particularly when some of the pieces are missing. In cases where parts of the inlay have been lost, their imprints sometimes remain on the glue line, or enough of the pieces survive to make a match.

In these cases the repairer should make a drawing by laying a sheet of tracing paper over the inlayed shape and carefully drawing along the imprint of the gluelines (if visible) and around the edge of the design. Laying the pencil side-on to the edge of the veneer produces an accurate 'rubbing' (the sharp dark line of lead from the pencil indicating the edge of the veneer). If a match can be made to an original design or other reference sources, a line drawing can be produced sufficient for fretsawing a new shell into the existing window.

This tutorial explains how to construct such a shell. The drawing is given in the Appendix. Make a photocopy of the drawing and cut a rectangle around it to the size of the veneers you use to build the pad (see steps 1 and 2 below).

BUILDING THE PAD

Chapter 1 explained the techniques of building a pad and fretsawing, so it is advisable to spend some time studying that chapter prior to starting this tutorial (see pp. 30–36).

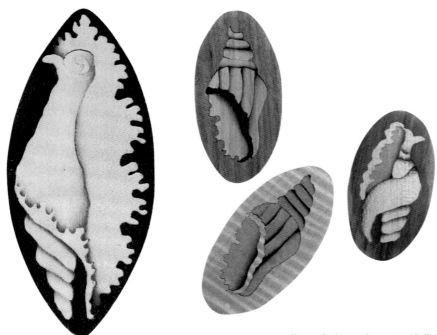

Figure 2: Some alternative shell designs

TOOLS REQUIRED

Hand fretsaw (machine type can also be used) with Swiss metal-
cutting 6/0 blade

Fretsaw table (see chapter 1 for instructions on making this)

Scalpel

Office stapler

Pin hammer

Small screwdriver

Silver sand, hot stove and pan

Mini bradawl (needle set into handle of a 4-jaw craft-knife holder)

MATERIALS REQUIRED

Sycamore, boxwood and poplar veneers, plus two wasters

Veneer tape (or 50-mm / 2-in wide parcel tape)

Paper glue

Paper design (line drawing)

Note that the tools, materials, method of building
the pad and the method of assembly is identical for
the patera design given in the next tutorial.

1 Cut sycamore, boxwood, poplar and 2 waster veneers,
larger than the size of the inlayed area by 25 mm (1 in)
in both directions. The grain for the four veneers should run
along the width of the oval inlay. Stick wide parcel tape
(or veneer tape) across the face sides of the poplar, boxwood
and sycamore veneers.

2 Place the poplar, boxwood and sycamore veneers
between the two wasters, making sure the taped sides
are facing you. Fasten them together at each corner with an
office stapler. The pins of the staples should face the bottom of
the pad. Paste the line drawing onto the top of the pad and
add a few more staples around the edges of the oval design to
give support to the pad. Hammer the pins of the staples flat
with a pin hammer. The pad is ready for fretsawing.

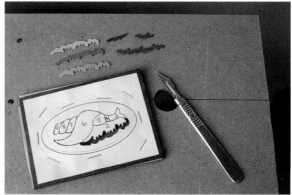

3 Using a sewing needle set into a 4-jaw craft-knife holder,
pierce a hole anywhere along the line of the piece to be
cut out. Insert the fretsaw blade from the back of the pad
following the loading technique detailed in *fretsawing* section of
chapter 1 (p. 34). If you have practised fretsawing, you should
be able to use a 6/0-size blade (the smallest) for this pad.
Otherwise use a 2/0 or 4/0 size. Cut the parts out in the
order in which they are numbered on the design. I have
fretsawn the most intricate piece (the wavy edge of the shell
opening) as cut No. I, as shown here.

4 Cut out No. 2 by cutting along the wavy line, turning the pad with one hand as you keep the fretsaw vertical to the cutting table. As you complete the wavy line, turn to cut the curved lines along the bottom of the body and neck of the shell. Remove the cut pieces and keep them safe.
By cutting in this sequence you are retaining most of the strength of the assembled pad for as long as possible. Separate the pad by removing the staples with a small electrical screwdriver.

5 Make a dry assembly with the untaped sides facing you. Use the boxwood for the background oval, the sycamore for the body of the shell and the poplar for the shell opening. This gives you an idea where the sandshading is required to provide the 3D animation. Take each piece in turn and sandshade the areas shown on the finished shell at step 6. Shade very, very lightly to obtain the natural effect—delicacy is of the essence here. (See the *Sandshading* section of chapter 1, p. 36, for details.) Do not worry if the protective paper curls up as you shade. It has already done its job by keeping the pieces intact during sawing.

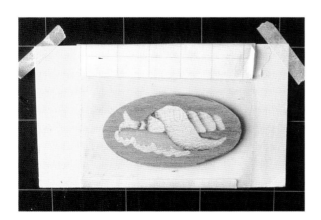

If you have used a 6/0-size blade to fretsaw the shell, the glue used to install the inlay will fill the gaps without trace. If you have used a blade thicker than 6/0 you may have to mix natural coloured grain filler with a little PVA glue and push it into the gaps with a spatula. The veneer tape on the face side prevents the filler escaping.

6 Cut a piece of gummed plastic bookbinding film, sticky side up. Stretch it across a piece of card. Lay the boxwood background veneer onto the sticky surface of the film, with the paper side facing you. Assemble the sandshaded pieces one by one, paper side up, to build the shell. Place veneer tape across the whole shell, then peel it away from the plastic film. Centralize the tracing paper template across the motif and cut along the oval line to complete the inlay.

TUTORIAL NO. 7: PATERA

Patera (plural: paterae) meaning a flat dish, first appeared in plaster moulds as a bas-relief in friezes. Circular dish-shaped casts of floral rosettes decorate ceilings and friezes in many stately homes across Europe. Circular and elliptical patterns were later introduced as a marquetry decoration and are now considered architectural features on neo-classical furniture.

Of all the patterns in this book, the patera is the perfect type for fretsaw work. It demands close control during sawing, together with the most delicate touch of sandshading to achieve the hollowed dish-shaped image. It is arguably the most impressive inlay motif of all and our experience has shown it to be the top choice with students.

The rosette, made up from 12 petals, requires 12 'blind' cuts to form the central vein of each petal. These cuts, which stop short of the ends of each petal, are known as accent lines and are an integral feature when fretsawing floral and foliage designs. The accent lines are artistically highlighted by backfilling with a coloured grain filler prior to gluing the motif to a baseboard.

Figure 1: Fretsawn patera

TOOLS REQUIRED

Hand fretsaw (machine type can also be used) with Swiss metal-
cutting 6/0 blade

Fretsaw table (see chapter 1 for instructions on making this)

Scalpel

Office stapler

Pin hammer

Small screwdriver

Silver sand, hot stove and pan

Mini bradawl (needle set into handle of a 4-jaw craft-knife holder)

MATERIALS REQUIRED

Sycamore veneer (rippled if available)

Magnolia veneer, plus 2 wasters

Boxwood veneer

Grain filler or pigment

Veneer tape (or 50-mm / 2-in wide parcel tape)

Paper glue

Paper design (see Appendix)

Book binding veneer and stiff card

If magnolia is not available, any contrasting but highly decorative veneer will suit, such as vavona burr, elm burr, kevasinga or pommelle. This veneer forms the background for the patera design. The rosette should be made using sycamore as the first choice, preferably with a ripple-effect figuring. Alternative choices are bird's-eye maple, ripple maple or poplar. Essentially, the rosette should be made from white or creamy-coloured veneer.

Note that a Hegner motorized fretsaw was used to cut this design. If you have not used the fretsaw before, please practise before attempting this design. Some schools and colleges do have these machines available for students' use. A 4/0-size blade was used to create the necessary gap in the accent lines. The hand-held fretsaw and table used to saw the shell (previous tutorial) is perfectly adequate for cutting this design.

To see how to assemble the pad and fretsaw the initial cuts, go to chapter 1: *Techniques* (p. 32).

1 First, cut out a petal. Next, cut out the tiny tip of the petal separately, as shown here on the fretsaw table.

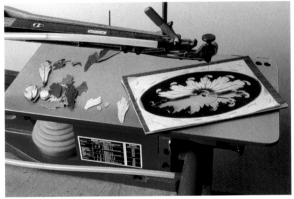

2 Remove the petals one by one, making sure you cut down the smaller accent lines that penetrate each side of the leaves. After removing a petal, remove the curled tip separately from the very end of the petal.

3 Separate the pad by removing the staples with the small screwdriver. Select the 12 sycamore petals and sandshade them as illustrated here. Be very careful not to overburn the tiny ends.

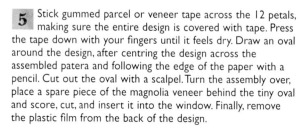

4 Lay a sheet of plastic bookbinding film across a stiff card and assemble the petals and their matching tips into the magnolia background. Don't worry about identifying which tip belongs to which petal. No two petals or tips of petals are alike and it quickly becomes obvious which window each one fits. Make sure the taped side of the assembly is facing you.

5 Stick gummed parcel or veneer tape across the 12 petals, making sure the entire design is covered with tape. Press the tape down with your fingers until it feels dry. Draw an oval around the design, after centring the design across the assembled patera and following the edge of the paper with a pencil. Cut out the oval with a scalpel. Turn the assembly over, place a spare piece of the magnolia veneer behind the tiny oval and score, cut, and insert it into the window. Finally, remove the plastic film from the back of the design.

6 Stringing: using a length of 1.5 mm ($^5/_8$ in) boxwood stringing, fit it around the circumference of the oval. Place the motif onto your cutting mat. Start in the centre of one *side* of the shape. Make elongated nicks with your scalpel into the inside edge of the stringer. This allows the stringer to bend into the oval edge without breaking. The nicks should penetrate more than half the width of the stringer and be spaced about 6 mm ($^1/_4$ in) apart. Put beads of PVA glue between the string and edge and rub dry after mating the two surfaces. Hold in place with masking tape.

7 To join the two ends together invisibly, place one end squarely on top of the other and make a 'scarf' joint. This is a diagonal cut made with the scalpel at a very acute angle. Cut through both stringers by pressing downwards on the scalpel. Remove the waste ends and bring the mating ends together with a spot of PVA. Tape and leave the assembly overnight to dry.

8 The final act is to bring life to the accent lines you created during the fretsawing. You need a pot of 'natural' (i.e. not coloured) grain filler and a dark pigment powder. We have used two colours here, Brown Umber and Raw Sienna, to obtain a mid-brown colour. The large piles of pigment are only for illustration. In reality you only need the tiniest 'pinch' mixed with the grain filler.

9 Spread the filler into the gaps of the petals. Work it in while the filler is soft, then scrape off any excess to leave a smooth surface. The veneer tape on the face side prevents the filler from escaping. That completes the patera. (Note that this picture was taken after the patera was cut into the gallery tray veneer described in chapter 5.)

PARQUETRY

Parquetry patterns are a product of cutting veneers into uniform shapes, consisting of straight lines cut at pre-determined angles. It is generally considered that parquetry developed after its characteristic shapes and arrangements were used on other types of application. The method of laying out geometric shapes, for instance, derived from the French word *parque*, first used by farmers and gardeners whose fields and flowerbeds were laid out in uniform shapes and sizes. The word also came to apply to a *parqueteur*, someone who laid uniform blocks in prescribed patterns to make interior floors.

In this section we have put together some traditional and proven patterns together with a relatively modern design to finish. Parquetry demands exactness, or the completed pattern will not work. Therefore, it is important to use the correct tools and equipment when preparing and cutting the veneers. To this end, we have returned to a method used during the 18th century for cutting parquetry stock. A simple mitre box and gents padsaw provides the means of producing accurately cut stock for the construction of precision parquetry. This method will be used on two of the designs: the Louis Cube and Chevron parquetry. After many years experimenting (and discarding) countless type of parquetry guillotines, both homemade and manufactured, we have thankfully resorted to the tried and tested mitre-box method. Once the angle is made in the mitre box, you know that every sawn piece will have precisely the same dimensions. You are advised to read the section on *Tools and Equipment: For Parquetry*, in chapter 1 (p. 9) for detailed instructions on how to construct the simple box and purchase the appropriate padsaw, if you don't already possess one.

Two basket-weave arrangements of contrasting patterns, but similar construction methods, provide an opportunity to apply sandshading to produce three-dimensional effects. Needless to say, the number of parquetry patterns is endless. This small but interesting selection will, we hope, feed your imagination and encourage further experimentation of your own.

Let us first, however, start your introduction to parquetry work by making the most basic and perhaps most used parquetry design in the world today: the chessboard.

Figure 1: The most widely used parquetry design, the chessboard

TUTORIAL NO. 8: CHESSBOARD

This is the most basic, yet most useful parquetry design of all. Whether you are constructing a chessboard to be used for international competition, where the squares have to be 50 mm (2 in) square, or making a miniature board to match pocket-sized chess pieces, the mode of construction remains the same. This tutorial assumes you are constructing a chessboard to international competition dimensions. Should you require a board of different dimensions, simply change the calculations given below to suit your own needs.

Please note that only metric measurements are used in this tutorial because parquetry demands accuracy and consistency. Providing approximate imperial equivalents alongside metric would only confuse the assembly.

First, calculate the size of the board or table by deciding on the size of one square; multiply by 8 to calculate the board's playing area; and add a border to each side to frame the chessboard.

USE THE FORMULA

Dimensions = (S x 8) + (B x 2) = L, where *S* = width of 1 square in mm; *B* = width of border in mm; and *L* = length of each side of the finished board, in mm.

Example: 1 square width = 50 mm
50 x 8 = 400 mm
border width = 75mm x 2 = 150 mm
length of each side = 550 mm

Early chessboards usually consisted of black and white squares. Today, we use many different veneers of contrasting colours with attractive grain and figure, giving a classical and pleasing appearance. The combination of veneers recommended for the two contrasting squares (dark veneer given first) are:

American walnut burr and masur birch
European walnut and ash burr
mahogany and sycamore

There are many more combinations you could try for yourself, or you can mix and match some of the above, as long as you achieve a clear contrast between the colours. Avoid using dyed veneers as they make a board look artificial and garish.

GRAIN DIRECTION

Parquetry relies on two basic elements for achieving symmetrical effects, namely: straight lines cut at predetermined angles, and direction of the grain. The latter is very important in constructing a chessboard. Five strips of one veneer are cut when only four are needed for the following reason: the direction of the grain and the figure should be continuous throughout the assembly. If we only cut four strips of each veneer, alternate lines of squares would have to be turned round 180° to achieve the staggered pattern. This means that the grain and figure would be lying in opposite directions on every other line. This can show a pronounced characteristic change in the appearance. Some veneers show this change more than others and it usually becomes more apparent when polish is applied. Reversing the angle of the grain and figure to the direction of light causes the change. Put this to the test yourself by taking two matching leaves of any veneer. Look at the face sides, then turn one veneer 180° without turning it over, and you can usually see the slight change in appearance. You can avoid this by cutting five strips of one veneer, which enables you to alternate the squares without having to reverse every other line.

TOOLS REQUIRED

Marquetry cutting board

Steel straight edge

Steel setsquare

Scalpel

MATERIALS REQUIRED

Dark veneer, 450 x 300 mm (5 strips)

Light veneer, 450 x 250 mm (4 strips)

Border, 600 x 350 mm

Veneer tape

Masking tape

1 Select two contrasting veneers, making sure they are slightly longer than the final board width and wide enough to get four strips from one of the veneers and five strips from the other (it doesn't matter which you use for which quantity). Cut two spacers from scraps of wood, both exactly the width of one square. Retain the strips in the order you have cut them. Number them 1–4 and 1–5 if it helps.

2 Alternate the strips as shown, securing the joints with veneer tape. Note that the short vertical lengths of tape should be put in place first, followed by long lengths covering the entire joint of two veneers. Make sure you wet the tape thoroughly to achieve good adhesion. Place the assembled strips up to the cutting board fence and line a steel setsquare to one edge. Cut the edge square with the scalpel.

3 Using the same two spacers and the steel straight edge, cut eight strips, again keeping them in the order you have cut them by numbering them 1–8. This is to retain the grain pattern throughout.

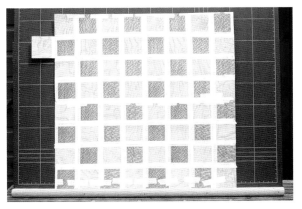

4 Turn all nine strips over, so that the untaped sides are facing you, but still in number order. Place strip 1 on the cutting mat, bring strip 2 up to it and stagger the squares one by one. Align the squares accurately so the joints continue in a straight line, not doglegged. Hold the strips in place temporarily with tabs of masking tape. When all eight strips are fixed, turn the assembly over to the taped side.

5 Hold the strips together with lengths of veneer tape. You now have two layers of tape, the second at 90° to the first layer. Cut off the protruding 9th squares from each side. That completes the playing area.

6 The central playing area can be glued to its baseboard before fitting the borders. To learn how to achieve this, follow the instruction for two-part pressing found in chapter 3 (follow the type A border, pp. 94–96).

TUTORIAL NO. 9: LOUIS CUBE

The Louis Cube received its name because it appeared on furniture in the late-17th and early-18th centuries during the reign of King Louis XIV of France (1643–1715). The design, however, was evident much earlier than this. The three-dimensional cube is a classical high-style parquetry design that has appeared on cabinetwork throughout France, Germany, Holland and England. Many derivatives of the name have emerged since that period, due to the use of the pattern on other handcrafts, such as fabrics, cross stitch and tapestry.

Three veneers of contrasting colour make up the design, with each veneer cut to the same size and at the same 60° angle. Setting the grain of the veneers in three different directions is the key to achieving the impressive three-dimensional image. It is therefore possible to create the image using just one veneer.

The most impressive combinations of veneer colours I have seen for this design are red, light brown and white. This in turn corresponds to veneers such as mahogany, boxwood and sycamore. The jewellery box shown in Figure 1 use sepele, anegré (aningeria) and sycamore.

Alternatively, you may want to experiment with three completely different veneers of your own

Figure 2: Close up detail of the Louis Cube design

choice. To calculate the quantity of each veneer needed, simply measure the area to be covered by the design and divide by three.

The size of the cubes should first be decided. In general furniture use, the smaller the cubes, the better the effect. As you increase the size the classic image is diluted until eventually it is lost altogether. Remember that each cube comprises three veneers cut into diamond shapes, each exactly the same size. The diamonds, which make up the three-sided cubes in the jewellery box shown in Figure 1, are 9 mm ($^3/_8$ in) wide. Let us assume you are to use that size in this tutorial.

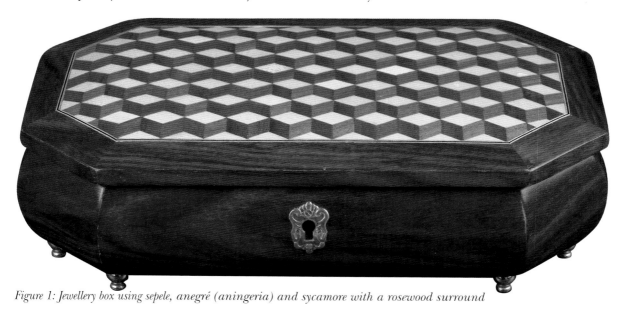

Figure 1: Jewellery box using sepele, anegré (aningeria) and sycamore with a rosewood surround

PREPARING THE CUBES

TOOLS REQUIRED

Mitre box

Gents padsaw

Dovetail saw

Sliding bevel

60° geometry set

Cutting board

Scalpel

Steel rule

Pencil

MATERIALS REQUIRED

Maple or sycamore veneers (size depending on design)

Mahogany or sepele veneers (size depending on design)

Boxwood or anegré veneers (size depending on design)

Cardboard sheet

Bookbinding film (see Suppliers, page 175)

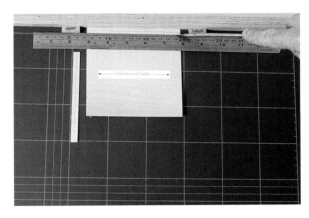

1 Using your marquetry cutting board and two identical spacers, cut strips about 150 mm (6 in) long from all three veneers, with the grain running along the length of each strip. Draw a pencil line along the length of each strip before cutting, to identify the direction of grain. The width of the spacers determines the width of each diamond.

Make sure you have constructed your mitre box (see p. 9) before proceeding to step 2.

2 To speed up sawing the diamonds, bunch about 6 strips together and tape them at one end. Make sure the pencil line on each strip in the bunch is facing upwards. Place the untaped end of the stack up to the gate of the mitre box, making sure all 6 strips are directly underneath each other, then saw through the stack. Repeat this for each of the three veneers that make up the design. Keep lifting the gate to clear sawdust from the mitre box, otherwise a build-up can cause inaccuracies.

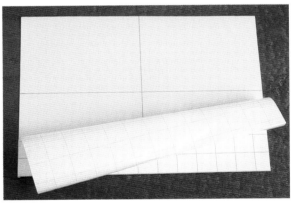

3 The materials you need to assemble the cubes are a piece of plain cardboard slightly larger than the size of the pattern and a roll of clear plastic gummed film, the sort used for bookbinding. Draw *xy* co-ordinates across the plain card as shown. Stretch plastic film across the card, securing it on the back with masking tape. The film's backing paper protects the gummed side and the parquetry when stored out of use. It also helps to keep your hands off the gummed surface when assembling the cubes.

4 Use the tip of the scalpel to pick up the first diamond piece (any colour) and place it onto the gummed paper, so that it sits across the *xy* co-ordinates of the card. Rest the heel of your hand on the turned-down backing paper to keep steady while positioning. Make sure the pencil lines on the diamond pieces are facing you.

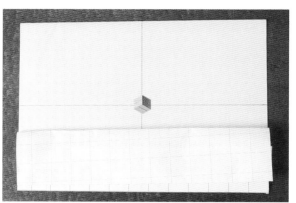

5 Place the other two colours, as shown, to complete the first cube. Note the three different directions of grain highlighted by the pencil lines. The point of the cube at which all three pieces converge should be sitting directly on top of the point where the *xy* lines cross. It is important to create uniformity of the design, left-to-right as well as top-to-bottom. Only by starting in the centre can this be achieved. If the cube does not fit perfectly together you have cut the angles wrong. Recheck your work now.

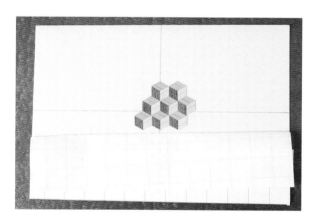

6 Working outwards towards the edges, build up the cubes, keeping an eye on the assembly and making sure it is kept square. Keep the joints tight and in-line. Remember that one error is multiplied in parquetry work, so take your time. Build the pattern larger than you need, so that, when trimmed to the final size, the outer edges will consist of half pieces, which should balance both left-to-right and top-to-bottom.

7 Note that the assembly is now ready to be cut to size. See how the pattern is balanced left-to-right and top-to-bottom, making the piece totally symmetrical. It may be advisable at this stage to rub a little PVA glue into the joints, but make sure only the tiniest amount is applied and well rubbed in. Note that the gummed film must stay on the face side until the assembly is glued to a baseboard (see p. 83).

For instruction on mounting and bordering, see chapter 3.

TUTORIAL NO. 10: BASKET WEAVE— RUSTIC TYPE

Basket weave parquetry offers two designs for furniture decoration. The rustic and the panel types are variations on the same theme and both need sandshading to illustrate the three-dimensional effect, but at the same time they are quite different in their final appearance. Their names offer some clue as to their appearance, the rustic having an Oriental look, while the panel design offers a more formal decorative option. The rustic design is an ideal pattern for decorating boxes, trays and small tables while the panel type, as the name suggests, provides a uniform panelled background on furniture to which other relief marquetry may be added.

Figure 1: Box with rustic type basket weave on the lid

Figure 2 Close-up detail of the rustic type design

TOOLS REQUIRED

Scalpel

Cutting board

Silver sand, hot stove and pan

Steel rule

MATERIALS REQUIRED

Anegré or boxwood veneer for the weave

Sepele veneer for the infill

Plastic bookbinding film (see suppliers list)

Cardboard

Note that the amount of veneer you need will depend on your project. In general, 80 per cent of the surface will be covered by the weave and 20 per cent by the infill.

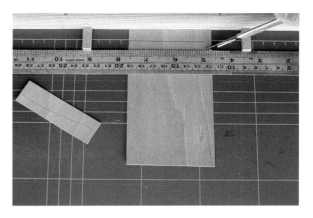

1 Make two spacers 18 mm (³/₄ in) long by 6mm (¹/₄ in) wide. Cut the weave veneer by cutting each sheet 75 mm (3 in) wide and 150 mm (6 in) long, with the grain running along the length. Using the marquetry cutting board and the 18 mm spacers, cut the veneer *across* the grain. Draw a pencil line along each strip as a marker to avoid veneer reversal during construction.

2 Sandshade both edges of each strip along the length. After sanding, slightly moisten the veneer by nipping a wet sponge with finger and thumb and running them down the strips. Stack the veneers between 2 scraps of wood, held together with a rubber band to prevent the strips from curling.

3 Turn the two spacers so that the 6mm (¹/₄ in) thickness is used. Place a sandshaded strip against the fence of the cutting board and, with a steel rule laid across the strip and the spacers, cut all the sandshaded strips into 6mm pieces. Note that you will be cutting *with* the grain this time. Let's get weaving!

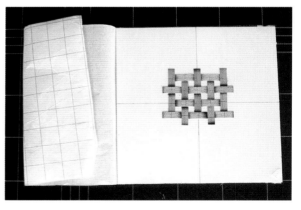

4 Find the centre of a sheet of cardboard, cut to the measurements suiting the panel you want to build. Stretch gummed plastic bookbinding film across the card and secure the film and its protective sheet to the bottom of the card with masking tape. Secure the film only at the top of the card, so that the protective sheet can be folded down as you stick veneers to the gummed surface.

It's important to build from the centre. That way, the pattern stays symmetrical to the panel you are filling. Try to keep the pieces as square to each other as possible as you lay them on the plastic sheet. Because the pieces are so small, it's not possible to be precise and you will find that the infill windows left by the weave will vary slightly in size. Don't worry unduly about this because, when the infill veneer is inserted, the difference in size adds to the final rustic appeal.

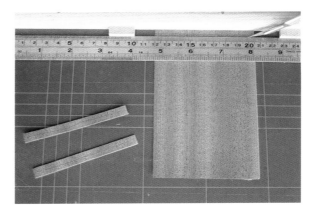

5 Cut strips of sepele (infill) about 150 mm (6 in) long and 6 mm (¹/₄ in) wide. The grain should run along the length.

6 Place the red insert strip into the infill window, scoring the veneer with the scalpel to make a good fit. Remove the strip, cut off the infill and insert it back into the window. Build up the pattern in this way laying first a few weaves, then a few infills.

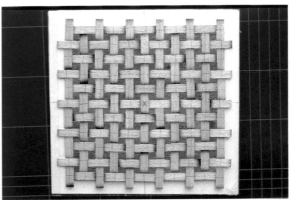

7 Finally, cut the completed panel to size, measuring from the central weave outwards in each direction. Make sure the assembly is cut square. The assembly is now ready for bordering and mounting (see chapter 3).

Remember that the gummed film remains on the assembly until it's pressed onto the baseboard. After pressing, remove the film (it simply peels off) leaving a layer of gum on the veneers. Cellulose thinners and a paper towel soon remove it.

TUTORIAL NO. 11: BASKET WEAVE— PANELLING TYPE

Another form of Basket weave parquetry is illustrated here. Like the first pattern, this still gives a weave appearance but takes on the look of a conventional interwoven panel. Only one veneer (boxwood or anegré) is needed for weaving the horizontal pattern, while the vertical infill consists of 1.5 mm ($^1/_{16}$ in) boxwood stringing. A steel or plastic set square is needed to keep the construction square, otherwise the tools and materials are the same as for the previous pattern. Construction is very similar to the first basket weave, except that the sandshaded strips are separated by stringers. This achieves the interwoven panelling appearance.

The tools and materials required are the same as for the rustic-type basket weave in tutorial no. 10 above.

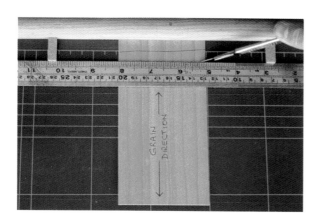

1 Make two wood spacers 18 mm ($^3/_4$ in) long and 6 mm ($^1/_4$ in) wide. Prepare veneer into sheets 75 mm (3 in) wide by 150 mm (6 in) long, with the grain running along the length. Using the marquetry cutting board, first cut strips 18 mm ($^3/_4$ in) wide, making sure you cut the veneer across the grain, as indicated. Draw a pencil line along each strip to avoid reversal during construction.

2 Sandshade both edges of the strips along their lengths. Don't overshade. After shading, moisten the veneers by nipping a wet sponge between finger and thumb and running them down the strip to dampen them (though don't over-wet them). Keep veneers in a pack between two scraps of wood, held together with a rubber band to stop them curling.

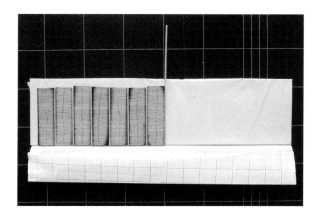

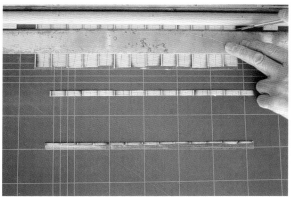

3 Cut a piece of cardboard to the size required for your application. Stretch plastic bookbinding film across the card, securing the film with masking tape. Place a sandshaded strip onto the gummed film (left-hand side) followed by a strip of 1.5 mm ($^1/_{16}$ in) stringing. Alternate along the length of the film, finishing with a stringer. Separate the assembly and its plastic film from the cardboard.

4 Place the assembly onto your cutting board and, using the two spacers set at 6-mm ($^1/_4$-in) widths, cut through the shaded strips, stringers and the plastic film. You must have a very sharp blade to do this, and make sure you press a bit harder than usual on the steel rule, which is holding the assembly in place. The extra pressure on the rule stops the veneers slipping on the plastic film during cutting.

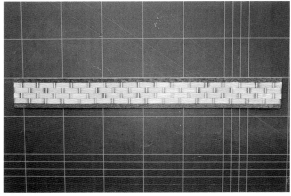

5 Place a second sheet of plastic film over the card used earlier. Place a steel rule across the film and position the first strip of weave up to the edge of the rule. Stagger the strips by half a weave to achieve the interwoven panelling effect. Strips can be joined up end-to-end to extend the pattern horizontally. (This is why we asked you to start with a shaded strip and end with a stringer at step 3.)

6 Border the panel weave to create a frame around the pattern. This type of basket weave makes ideal decoration for the rim around a gallery tray or panels around the sides of the box in our example. You will note there are two layers of gummed film on the face side of the veneers. These must stay on until the assembly is glued to a baseboard. The films easily pull off. See chapter 3 for the details on bordering and mounting a panel.

TUTORIAL NO. 12: CHEVRON

This is an ideal design for bordering furniture or fittings within the home. I first came across this pattern during a guided tour of Spenfield House, Leeds, built in 1876 and now a Grade 2 listed building owned by a hotel chain. The ground floor living and drawing rooms display a great deal of exquisite marquetry work of the Robert Adam and his brothers (John, James and William) style. On the grand, winding 12-foot wide staircase leading to the first floor, the ornate mahogany banister rails on both sides of the staircase have chevron parquetry inlaid into the solid wood. In total, counting both banisters and two landings, there are over 60 m (200 ft) of inlaid chevrons. Each chevron measures only 6 mm (¹/₄ in) in width, which means that over 10,000 chevrons had to be cut, assembled and inlaid. The architect for this building was George Corson, who was responsible for constructing the Grand Theatre in Leeds city centre. Sadly, local historians have no record of the craftsmen who constructed any of this work.

Chevron parquetry gives a three-dimensional effect and is immediately impressive. It is also great fun building the core from which the chevrons are cut and assembled. Perhaps that is why the design was chosen for such a large construction. The choice of designs is endless, since you can select your own colour combination, as well as the size and number of veneer pieces that make up the core strip—in short, you can simply let your imagination run free. The greater the number of pieces laid into the core, the more impressive the chevrons become.

As you can see from Figure 1, long narrow surfaces make ideal locations for such a design. You may want to consider applying it to the rim of the oval gallery tray project in chapter 5. The picture here shows chevron parquetry placed around the outside rim of a rectangular gallery tray, which was made in the year 2000. A total of about 1.8 m (6 ft), which equates to cutting 288 chevrons, was needed to decorate the tray shown on p. 97. This seemed a huge challenge at the time, but it soon came together and the time spent building, cutting and assembling was worth it in the end. The scale of this task, however, pales into insignificance when compared to the 10,000 chevrons our unnamed craftsmen made over 120 years ago.

The following tutorial shows two patterns being assembled. The first is the pattern for the oval gallery tray project in chapter 5. The second we applied to the jewellery box, also in chapter 5. You may wish to select your own veneers and create your own core strip, and we would encourage you to do so. The method of construction remains the same, except that the first pattern is cut at a 60° angle, and the second is cut at 45°.

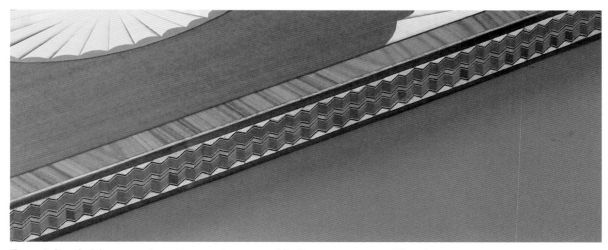

Figure 1: Detail of the rectangular gallery tray shown on p. 97. Chevrons were cut at 60° angle.

DESIGN FOR THE OVAL GALLERY TRAY

TOOLS REQUIRED

Scalpel

Marquetry cutting board

Steel rule

Mitre box

Gents padsaw

Cutting board

60° angle square

45° angle square

Sliding bevel

MATERIALS REQUIRED

Gallery tray veneers: zebrano, dyed green and sepele

Jewellery box veneers: yew, ash burr and sepele, plus a commercial
   decorative banding

Veneer tape (or 50 mm / 2 in wide parcel tape)

Plastic bookbinding film (see Suppliers. p. 175)

Sheet of card

1 The circumference of the oval gallery tray is approximately 1.5 m (5 ft). Allowing for a spare strip, cut 12 strips of zebrano veneer 6 mm (¼ in) wide (make two spacers that width) and about 300 mm (12 in) long, with the grain running with the length.

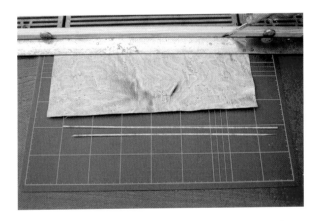

2 Using two £1 coins (or other coins 3 mm thick each) stood edgeways on as spacers, cut 6 strips of dyed mid/dark green veneer. The grain runs with the length.

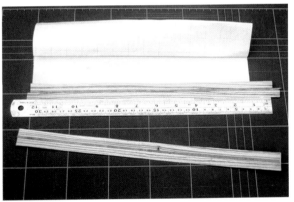

3 Tape a 300 mm (12 in) length of gummed plastic bookbinding film to a sheet of card. Place the rule along the length and assemble two layers of zebrano with a strip of green veneer as the sandwich. Stick parcel or veneer tape to the side facing you, then peel it off from the plastic film. Assemble all 6 strips in this fashion using the same plastic film.

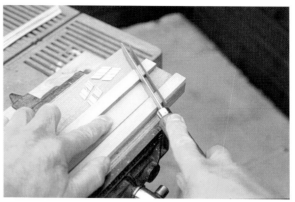

4 Using the mitre box (as detailed on p.9), cut chevrons at 60° angles, 6 mm ($^1/_4$ in) wide. First cut the chevrons with the un-taped side of the strip facing you. Cut three 300 mm (12 in) strips this way, as illustrated. It is much safer to place the mitre box in a vice when sawing the chevrons. Keep blowing the sawdust away from the gate, to prevent build-up changing the angle.

5 Now saw three strips with the taped side facing you. This will create an opposite angle to the first cuts, which will form the chevrons.

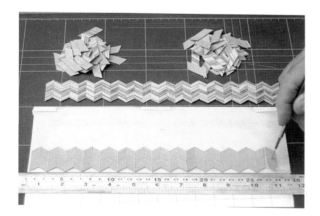

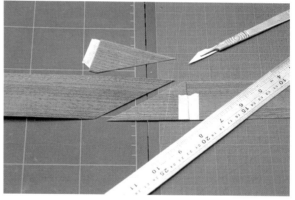

6 Place a rule along the gummed plastic film to act as a straight edge. Place cut chevrons, taped side up, onto the film. Make two piles of chevrons, one from the first cut, the other from the second. Alternate the laying as you build the strips. You will just be able to see through the parcel tape enough to confirm that the pattern matches. When the strip is assembled lay another length of parcel or veneer tape across the strip. Remove from the film and build the rest.

7 Now to border the chevrons. First measure the width of the area you want to decorate and add 6mm ($^1/_4$ in). For the gallery tray rim you need about 1.5 m (5 ft). To make this in one length join short strips together with a scarf joint, as shown. Overlap the ends by about 50 mm (2 in) and make a diagonal cut through both veneers.

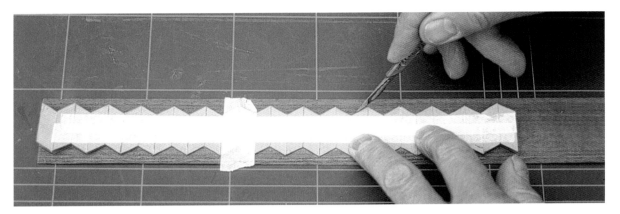

8 For illustration purposes only, I have shown the border veneer without any veneer tape added. It is, however, vital that tape is placed across the outer edges of the red veneer to prevent the points of the triangles breaking as you backcut the chevrons into the border. Centre the chevrons on the border veneer and, using the scalpel, score around the triangles that form the edges of the chevrons.

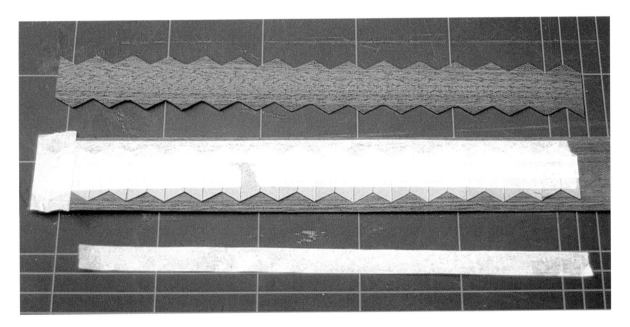

9 Cut through the scored line. Remove the window and insert the chevron strip. Tape it in place with veneer tape. Please note that for illustration purposes I have again not shown tape placed on the border veneer—don't forget to put it on at step 8. Now continue laying the remaining strips, by joining them onto the ends of the previously laid strip.

See the gallery tray project in chapter 5 for instructions on gluing the strip to the rim.

As you approach the last few inches of the gallery rim, measure the distance left to be covered and see if the 6mm (¼ in) chevrons will divide equally into the space. If they do, well done. If they don't, cut the last few chevrons either slightly bigger or smaller than the norm (though by no more than 1 mm). To achieve this, remove the gate on the mitre box and calculate (by eye) how much bigger or smaller each cut needs to be. If you restrict the changes to no more than 1 mm it will not be noticeable to the eye.

DESIGN FOR THE JEWELLERY BOX

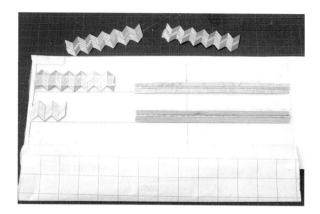

1 The method of construction follows the previous chevron assembly, with the exception that different woods are used for building the core, and the chevrons are cut at 45°.

Cut 4 strips of yew about 300 mm (12 in) long and 6 mm (¹/₄ in) wide (grain with the length). For our sandwich we used a strip of purchased banding between the strips of yew, as shown. It consists of five veneers, arranged white/black/white/black/white. You could make your own simply by gluing together 5 veneers, in the order given, and cut them on a bandsaw to about 1 mm thick. Assemble the strips as shown following steps 1–3 of the previous tutorial.

2 Set up a 45° angle cut on the mitre box (as detailed on p. 9) and cut chevrons 6 mm (¹/₄ in) wide. Saw two strips with the veneers facing you and two with the taped side facing you. This produces the opposite angles to make the chevron shape. (Picture shows samples of both angles.)

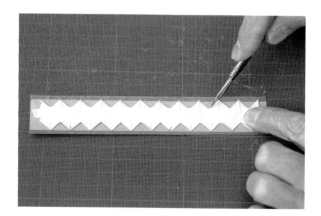

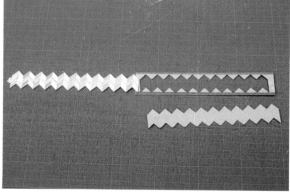

3 Place veneer tape across the border veneer so that the points of the triangles don't break. Lay the chevrons centrally on the border veneer and score around the edges.

4 Remove the chevrons and cut out the window. Insert chevrons into the window and secure with veneer tape. Repeat for each of the eight panels needed around the box lid. (for layout see the jewellery box project in chapter 5). That completes the chevron assembly.

MOUNTING, PRESSING AND BORDERING

Applying marquetry work to furniture requires a degree of technical know-how mixed with artistic flair. Consideration should be given to the choice of veneers, the harmony of the marquetry with the furniture, and finally, the symmetrical and balanced appearance of the whole piece. The first two elements have already been covered in chapter 2, when you constructed your chosen marquetry design. This chapter shows you how to mount and border that work to produce a panel worthy of inclusion in your furniture. The final presentation of the decorated panel is the prime object of discussion in this chapter, whether it be a picture, table top, drawer front, cupboard door or a feature set into a firescreen.

MOUNTING

There are two ways to mount a central marquetry panel to its groundwork and both are illustrated in this chapter. One method is to add the borders after mounting and pressing the central panel and, for assemblies that are square or rectangular in shape, this method will be recommended. The other method is to add the borders to the central panel before mounting and pressing, then glue the whole assembly in one go. This method must be used on circular and elliptical shapes because it is not possible to match the same radius once the panel is glued in place.

COUNTERBALANCING VENEER

In most cases, today's choice of groundwork for mounting marquetry work is Medium Density Fibreboard (MDF). This is chosen because its man-made composition removes the problem of future movement that natural timber boards present, particularly in modern, centrally heated homes. However, this should not mislead you into thinking that movement will not occur when a veneered assembly is first glued to an MDF board. Cupping of the board (bending outwards to one side) will almost certainly occur unless an equal and opposite counter-balancing veneer is glued to the reverse side of the board at the same time. In veneering work, it is normal practice to apply a counter-balancing veneer to the back of the groundwork.

Figure 1: A well-balanced panel

STRINGING, BANDING AND BORDERING

A selection of both standard and challenging border arrangements is illustrated below, but first some definitions of the materials available for making up borders need to be given.

STRINGING

What's in a name? To clarify the matter so as not to cause confusion at some future date, this product is known by marqueteurs as stringing (generally) or stringers (the individual pieces). It is also catalogued by some retail outlets as 'lines', but in the furniture-making industry it is always called 'inlays'. In all cases, there are two types: flat and square. They are usually made from boxwood (*buxus sempervirens*), chosen because of its straight, dense grain. The flat stringing has a veneer thickness of 0.7 mm, whereas the square is, as the name implies, the same thickness as the width. In each case, they are available in either white or dyed black, and sold in one-metre lengths, in

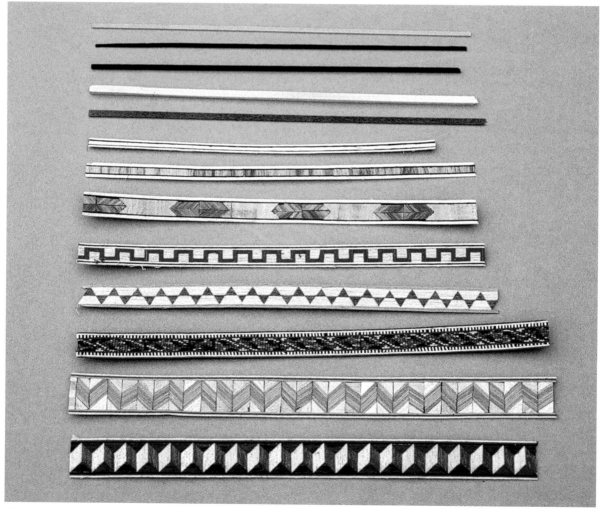

Figure 1: A mixture of commercial and home-made bandings

widths of 1 mm, 1.5 mm, 1.8 mm, 2.7 mm and 3.4 mm. Occasionally, square stringing can be obtained in other dyed colours (most often red, blue and green) as well as in ebony and rosewood.

The square version is used where a thin line is added to an already veneered panel, and a narrow line needs to be inserted (inlayed) for decoration. A router chases out a channel in the veneer and groundwork to a depth slightly less than the thickness of the square stringing. The stringing is glued into the channel, then sanded to the level of the surrounding veneer work. Another typical application of square stringing would be for restoration of a broken inlay.

In all the projects and tutorials given in this book, only flat stringing is used.

BANDING

This is a narrow strip of decoration comprising two or more contrasting woods. A simple banding can easily be constructed by gluing together three sheets of veneer, where one sheet is black and the other two white. Apply PVA glue to one side of each white veneer and make sure the grain of each veneer is running in the same direction, then place the black sheet between the two white sheets. Press the glued sheets for an hour. The resulting

white/black/white 'sandwich' can be cut into thin strips (along the grain) about 1 mm wide, using a scalpel and steel rule. Bandings made any wider than this would have to be cut on a band saw.

BORDERING ARRANGEMENTS

We have included four examples of bordering arrangements that are typical of the types used in furniture making. The first two examples can be fitted after the central panel is mounted and pressed, but the last two must be fitted *before* mounting and pressing.

First, we need to examine our method of two-stage pressing. For panels without curved edges (squares and rectangles) two-stage pressing offers distinct advantages to fitting borders and stringers. First, the panel (with perhaps its marquetry work already in place) is centred permanently in place; second, you are able to install borders and stringers in the knowledge that the mitred joints will be aligned correctly. However, this second advantage depends on producing a groundwork that is perfectly square. A bench saw with an accurate fence produces a square panel without a problem. For hobbyists who may not have access to one, most DIY suppliers of MDF will cut the panel for you.

Figure 2: Home-made three-core banding cut with a scalpel

TWO-STAGE PRESSING

STAGE 1

The key to success in the first stage is to be able to remove a veneered panel from a cold press after only a few minutes pressing in order to cut and remove surplus veneer from around the edges before the veneer becomes immovably stuck to the groundwork. Experience has shown that 10 minutes is an appropriate time for the first stage of pressing, providing standard PVA glue is used. Other proprietary brands that offer rapid setting times may require shorter durations.

The term 'cold press' is used advisedly, because this method of mounting and bordering will not work if a heated press is used. In a heated press, the veneer will bond permanently to its groundwork in less than 1 minute, making it difficult to remove veneer without possible damage to the groundwork.

Two-stage pressing provides an opportunity to work outwards from the centre. This way, the tasks are broken down to manageable proportions, giving you complete control over each stage.

1 Mark *xy* co-ordinates across the groundwork and the panel you wish to mount. Align the panel centrally and place in the press for 10 minutes only.

2 Set the cutting gauge to the width of the border you have decided on for the finished panel. Cut through the veneer on each side. Peal off the veneers with a sharp chisel or scalpel, at the same time scraping away the glue from the groundwork. Return the work to the press for an hour. The panel is now 'square to the board', and providing the board was cut square to start with, stage 2 becomes easier to manage.

STAGE 2

The second stage involves fitting borders, stringer and / or decorative banding. This stage becomes very manageable now the central panel is permanently in place. Once you have decided on the type of border (see below), cut, fit and hinge the parts with veneer tape, then cut the mitres before gluing and pressing. Figure 1 illustrates the taping and hinging arrangement, together with the method of applying PVA glue to each border in turn, before pressing the whole border assembly.

Figure 1: Stage 2, bordering arrangement

BORDERING STYLES

TRADITIONAL 'IN-LINE' BORDER

In general, the outer border should be approximately 4 times wider than the inner border with ratios like 25 mm (1 in) outer border to 6 mm ($^1/_4$ in) inner border. Separate the two with a 1.5 mm stringer. The chessboard shown right illustrates the standard single-stringing border arrangement.

TOOLS REQUIRED

Scalpel

Spacers (cut to size)

Steel straight edge

Cutting board

MATERIALS REQUIRED

Veneers of your choice

Veneer tape

1.5 mm Stringing

Using pre-prepared spacers, cut 4 strips for the outer border, making them 25 mm (1 in) longer than needed. Repeat the same procedure by cutting 4 strips for the inner border. Make sure you have allowed enough extra width on the outer border to overlap the edges of the panel.

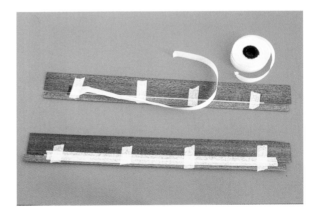

1 Place a strip of 1.5 mm stringing between the two borders and hold tightly together with veneer tape applied to the face side. Lay short tabs of tape *across* the joints first, then lay one long length over the joints as illustrated.

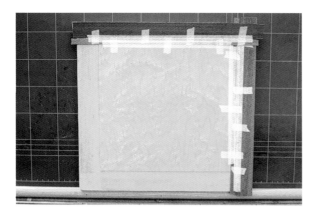

2 Place one assembled border strip up to the edge of the mounted work, making sure the stringer and border veneers overlap at each end. Hold in place with veneer tape as shown. Repeat for the other three sides.

3 Place veneer tape along the lines where the mitres are to be cut, making sure you tape both the top and the underneath border. This is important because it prevents the veneers splitting when you cut the mitres.

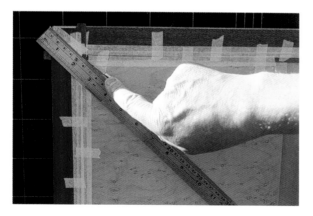

4 Turn the panel over and carefully cut through the overhanging veneers on the corner. This exposes the corner that you could not see before. Turn the panel back to the face side and line up the steel rule between the outer corner and where the two inner borders cross and meet each other. Hold the rule firmly with one hand while you cut through both layers of veneer and both stringers. Make a light cut first, followed by firmer cuts, until you feel the knife penetrate both layers. Remove the waste veneers and stringers.

5 You should have perfect mitres every time, with the stringers meeting each other squarely.

BOOK-MATCHED CROSSBANDING

Crossbanding is the classic bordering arrangement for furniture panels, cabinet doors, drawer fronts, end panels and so on. Note that the direction of the grain points to the centre of the panel, lying at 90° to the stringer. Also note the book-matched pattern at each corner.

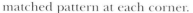

Figure 1: Crossbanding book-matched at four corners

TOOLS REQUIRED:

Same as for the Traditional 'In-line' Border

MATERIALS REQUIRED

Veneer with distinct stripy figure, such as kevasinga

Brazilian rosewood (see picture)

Veneer tape

1.5 mm stringing (white or dyed black)

1 The objective is to achieve a mirror image, or book-match, at each corner. Take one of the border pairs you have cut and place them up to a corner, one on each side. Don't reverse or turn around either of the strips, but keep them as you cut them from the leaf.

Take note of a distinctive stripe (arrows) which appears on both veneers. Measure and mark in pencil where the distinctive stripe appears on both sides of the corner and line up the stripe to those marks. Tape the veneers in place with veneer tape. Repeat for the other three corners.

Place veneer tape along both veneers where you are going to cut the mitres. This protects the corners. Place a steel rule and cut through both veneers to make the mitre. Repeat for each corner.

Finally, where the strips overlap in the centres of each side, cut through both veneers to create an invisible joint. Brazilian rosewoods make a good effect for this type of border.

QUARTERED CORNERS AND CROSSBANDING

This arrangement is currently the most traditional method of bordering panels on cabinet work. Due to its curved corners, this bordering arrangement has to be fitted *before* pressing the central panel.

TOOLS REQUIRED

Same as for the Traditional 'In-line' Border, *plus* a compass

MATERIALS REQUIRED

Sepele veneer

1.5 mm boxwood stringing

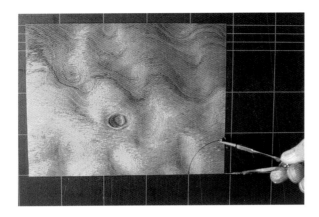

1 Draw a semi-circle to a radius that balances the panel. Cut round the line with a scalpel and remove the corner. Place sepele crossbanding and a 1.5 mm stringer along each side leading up to the corner, leaving an overhang of stringer on each corner.

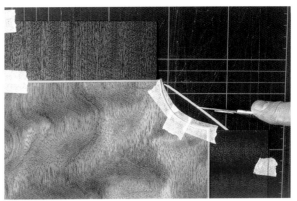

2 Cut a short length of stringer to fit around the curved corner, first making elongated cuts to the inside of the stringer, as shown on a spare sample. The cuts should penetrate two-thirds of the width of the stringer and be about 6 mm (¹/₄ in) apart. Glue with PVA and tape the stringer tight up to the curved edge with masking tape. Mitre the two corners where the stringers cross. Leave for minimum of two hours to dry.

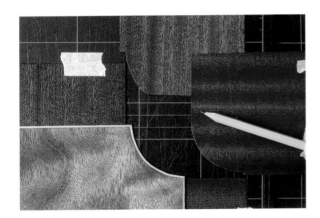

3 Cut two pieces of sepele, each large enough to cover the entire corner. Use the curved stringer as a template to score and cut the curved radius and the corners. Cut one piece for the left side and the other for the right. Tape them in place with veneer tape. Masking tape was used here for illustration purposes only.

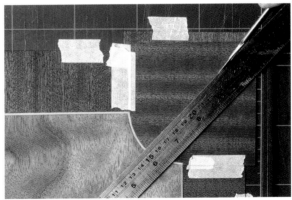

4 Find the centre of the curve (45°); line up a steel rule and cut through both veneers with the scalpel to make a mitred joint.

RADIUS CROSSBANDING

This border arrangement has to be fitted before pressing the central panel. The gallery tray project in chapter 5 is used for this illustration.

TOOLS REQUIRED

Same as for the Traditional 'In-line' Border

MATERIALS REQUIRED

Stripy veneers: sepele, kevasinga, walnut

Veneer tape

1.5 mm stringer (white or dyed black as preferred)

The crossbanding border surrounds the central panel, with the grain lying 90° to the direction of the stringer.

Fit a 1.5 mm stringer plus crossbanding to the outer edge of the tray with small strips of sepele. The two operations are carried out together. Both sides of the tray have to be completed in the same way. For each side, two lengths of 1.5 mm stringer are required as well as a number of 100 x 50 mm (4 x 2 in) strips of sepele veneer to make the crossbanding. The grain should run with the 50 mm (2 in) width. To assist bending the stringer, make elongated cuts about every 10 mm (³/₈ in) to the inside edge, as per the patera assembly in chapter 2 (p. 73).

1 Place a strip of sepele (note the grain pointing towards the centre of the tray) under the stringer and the tray veneer. Tape in place with tabs of masking tape. Score the sepele along the line where it meets the stringer, using the edge of the stringer as a template.

2 Where the sepele overlaps the previously laid piece, place a steel rule and cut through both pieces at the same time, to form an invisible joint.

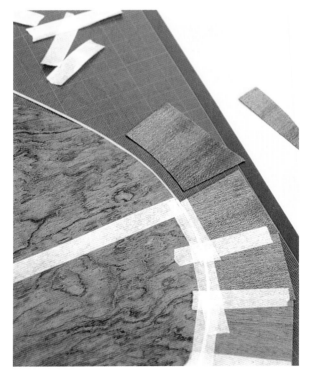

3 Remove the surplus veneer and tape the piece of sepele in place with veneer tape. Continue around the circumference in this fashion. No glue is necessary because the veneer tape (placed on the face side) holds the assembly tight. To join two lengths of stringer together and to complete the joint when the end meets the start, you need to make a scarf joint. Lay one stringer squarely on top of the other and make a very acute elongated cut through both stringers. This is best done by pressing straight down with the knife, rather than pulling the knife across the wood. Go to chapter 5: *Gallery Tray*, to complete the project.

SANDING AND FINISHING

K nowledge, care, patience and time are the key factors in producing a finish worthy of any eye-catching marquetry and cabinetwork. The information offered in this chapter deals with the techniques you should attain to put the finishing touches to your work. To this end, please use this chapter as a foundation for learning the skills which stretch beyond the boundaries of this book.

TOOLS REQUIRED

Orbital palm sander (Quarter or sixth sheet size.)

Cork sanding block

Steel rule

Vacuum cleaner with hand-brush attachment

Lacquer brush

Polishing mop

Polishing rubber (mouse in the US)

Dust mask

MATERIALS REQUIRED

Wire wool, grade 0000

Roll of paper towel

Sandpapers

    Aluminium oxide, 80 grit and 120 grit

    Garnet paper, 240 grit

    Silicon Carbide finishing paper, 320 and 400 grit

    Wet or dry finishing paper, 600 grit and 1200 grit

Polishes

    Cellulose sanding sealer

    Shellac sanding sealer

    French polish (transparent)

    Polyurethane clear varnish

    Burnishing cream

    Beeswax

    Renaissance wax polish

    Cellulose thinners

    Methylated spirit

    White spirit

Figure 1: Tools and polishes

CLEANING

Before you can apply finishing materials to your marquetry or parquetry work, the veneers must first be cleaned and then sanded. We distinguish between the two processes even though sanding is itself a form of cleaning.

The cleaning process requires removal of any veneer tape that has been left on during the mounting and pressing processes covered in chapter 3.

REMOVAL OF VENEER TAPE

Removing veneer tape is the reverse process of applying it. You simply wet it and wait about 2 minutes for the paper to soften, after which time it can be pushed off the veneer using the end of a steel rule. Where two or more layers of tape exist, a second wetting will be necessary.

Avoid wetting the untaped surfaces of surrounding veneers because excess water can cause the veneers to blister. Use your finger to direct the water exactly where you need it.

CELLULOSE SANDING SEALER

Sanding sealer is used to seal the woods to prevent leaching or bleeding. This is where the dust from one veneer can penetrate into adjacent veneers, causing permanent discolouring. It can occur during two of the finishing processes—both when sanding and when applying the finishing material, such as a lacquer. Most veneers will not leach at all, but those that do can contaminate white or light-coloured veneers used in the assembly. Two veneers that always leach are African ebony (black dust) and padauk (red dust). Some rosewoods leach oil, and dyed veneers can sometimes leach their dye. If the above-named woods have not been used, it is generally safe to commence sanding without the protection of sanding sealer. If you are in doubt and once the tapes have been cleaned off, apply a coat of cellulose sanding sealer, leaving about 15 minutes drying time. This raises the grain but also seals it to prevent leaching. African ebony and padauk may need more than one coat.

Figure 2: Removing veneer tape from a pressed panel

SANDING

There are a number of methods available to make a marquetry/parquetry panel 'flat' in readiness for accepting a finish. The term 'flat' means that all veneers have been sanded to the same thickness, all dirt, glue and gum marks from the veneer tape have been totally removed and the surface is pristine clean.

Unless you achieve total flatness at the sanding stage, no amount of finishing material will compensate.

METHOD 1: RANDOM ORBITAL SANDING

This method, used by most professional woodcrafts workers, offers the quickest and most acceptable results. It does, however, have one major drawback for the inexperienced: it is all too easy to sand through the veneers. Therefore, knowing when to stop sanding is vital to this process. It is advisable to practise on spare veneered panels to get acquainted with the sander and the speed with which the papers remove the waste material. Once you have confidence with the technique, you will find a random orbital sander totally invaluable in all your veneer work.

The advantage of using a random orbital sander is that it gives an even 'key' across the surface. This is because the action of the sander, as the name suggests, orbits front-to-back and side-to-side simultaneously. Generally, sanders come in three sizes, and are usually identified by the size of paper they hold. These are: quarter sheet, third sheet and sixth sheet (see Figure 3), the measurements being a proportion of a full sheet of A4 measuring 297 x 210 mm ($11^{3}/_{4}$ x $8^{1}/_{4}$ in). The quarter and sixth sheet sizes are classed as 'palm sanders' because they fit in the palm of your hand. It is advisable to use these in preference to the larger third sheet size because they offer more control, allowing you to work on small areas at a time as you sand across a panel.

Safety Some random orbital sanders have a plastic 'skirt' surrounding the paper and take a vacuum cleaner attachment—much preferable because it allows dust-free sanding. Others incorporate a dust bag, which collects some of the dust. For your health's sake, you should always wear a facemask when sanding.

Load the palm sander with a sheet of 80-grit aluminium oxide paper, indicated on the back of the paper as P80. It is usually best to start sanding from one corner, working along the length of the panel in the general direction of the grain. Slightly overlap the previously sanded area, but make sure the sander does not hang over the edge of the panel by more than $^{1}/_{4}$ of its width.

Figure 3: $^{1}/_{4}$, $^{1}/_{2}$ and $^{1}/_{6}$ sheet orbital sanders

Figure 4: Orbital sander and vacuum attachment

Watch for the surface to come clean and flat. Move across the panel one area at a time. Keep stopping and cleaning the surface area with the hand brush attachment of the vacuum cleaner. Feel with your fingers for flatness and look for any remaining dirt. You can press a bit harder on the sander if a stubborn area of dirt persists, but only press for two or three seconds. With P80 paper it should only take about two minutes to sand a panel 600 x 600 mm (2 x 2 ft) 'flat' and 'clean'. This is a good benchmark to measure against and should prevent you from oversanding. If a balancing veneer has been glued to the reverse of the panel, sand that in the same manner.

The rough surface produced by the 80-grit paper will need smoothing out slightly and a final sanding with 120-grit aluminium oxide paper leaves just enough 'key' for the finishing materials to bond to.

Sand the balancing veneer on the back of the panel first, followed by sanding the face side. This time it only takes a couple of 'swift passes' across the panel to smooth out the rough surface. Only ten seconds of sanding each side of a board the size mentioned above is sufficient to achieve the necessary key.

At this stage, be careful not to touch the surface with your fingers because it is 'pristine clean and flat', and your fingers may contaminate the surface. If you have to touch it, use the heel of your hand.

Clean off the surface of the panel with the vacuum brush attachment and immediately apply one coat of cellulose sanding sealer using a lacquer brush. Leave to dry for $\frac{1}{2}$ hour and apply a coat to the balancing veneer. This is always an exciting moment, because you will see, for the first time, the beauty of the colours in the marquetry work and surrounding veneers you have toiled over. Lightly sand the raised grain with 400-grit silicon carbide paper. The surface is now ready for a finishing material.

METHOD 2: HAND SANDING

The order of this process almost mirrors that of random orbital sanding, with the exception that 80-grit paper is not used. The reason for this is that 80-grit used with a cork sanding-block and rubbed across veneers manually will most certainly produce deep scratches that will prove almost impossible to remove. Instead, 120-grit paper, wrapped around a cork sanding-block and diligently used, will produce the required results.

Sand the balancing veneer on the reverse of the panel first, followed by the face side. Sand in the general direction of the grain, applying even pressure on the cork block. Using your fingers, keep checking for flatness and cleanliness. Keep stopping and remove the dust with the vacuum brush attachment, then examine the surface critically. When the entire surface looks clean and flat, *stop sanding*. Apply one coat of sanding sealer to both sides of the panel. Lightly sand the raised grain with 400-grit silicon carbide paper.

Figure 6 shows, from the top, wet or dry paper, silicon carbide paper, 80-grit and 120-grit aluminium oxide papers.

Figure 5: Sanding with 120-grit paper provides a 'key'

Figure 6: ¼ sheet papers to fit a sanding block

FINISHING

Essentially, furniture is finished with a proprietary polish to protect it and to emphasize the natural colours and figuring in the woods. When marquetry is included, it is essential to select a finish that will retain the natural colours of the woods used in the design. We therefore try to select materials that are transparent, or that dry transparent. For each of the projects included in this book, a variety of finishes are described, with advice on their appropriate application.

Finishing can only effectively be carried out in warm conditions. Cold and damp are totally alien to all polishing materials and should be avoided.

Safety Always keep polishes away from heat sources and out of direct sunlight. Apply the materials in a well-ventilated area, as some of the products emit toxic odours. Keep the work area free of dust.

LACQUERS

Pre-catalysed Lacquer This is an easy-to-apply, ready-mixed lacquer that may be applied by brush, or sprayed on after being thinned with cellulose thinners to a ratio recommended by the manufacturer. Further coats can be applied every two hours. Usually, two to five coats provide enough 'body' for rubbing back with 1200 grit wet or dry emery paper and 0000 grade wire wool. 'Pre-cat' lacquers are usually only available in large quantities and have a short shelf life, making them suitable only for trade and colleges where high usage warrants buying them.

French 'Transparent' Polish Previous experience is needed to work with this finishing material. Dedicated students should seek tuition. Made from the finest bleached de-waxed shellac, transparent polish produces a finish of high clarity, ideal for marquetry work. This alcohol-based product can either be applied with a polishing mop or a rubber (known as a mouse in the United States). Multiple layers build up the all-important 'body' of polish. It is an appropriate material for classic high-style furniture, such as the pier table.

Polyurethane 'Clear' Varnish This is by far the easiest of finishes to apply and ideal for surfaces that need to be water-resistant or protected from knocks. The white-spirit-based 'clear varnish' is available in matt, satin or gloss finishes. As directed on the tin, this product slightly mellows the woods, giving a classic 'antique' appearance. The gallery tray and chessboard shown in this book were coated with this product, and the mellow appearance, we feel, enhanced the finished effect. A very durable finish, it offers maximum protection against knocks and scratches. Brushed-on coats dry in four hours, and three coats normally provide enough body for most surfaces. Rub back between coats with 400 grit silicon carbide paper, using an orbital palm sander if available, followed by 0000 grade wire wool.

Beeswax Available in white or coloured for dark woods. Ideal for applying on top of sanding sealer. Protects against spillages and produces a satin finish if applied with 0000 grade wirewool.

Figure 1: Bring out the colours

Figure 2: The final touch.

Renaissance Wax Polish This polish is white and dries transparent, but offers much more moisture-resistance than other wax products. It protects against spillage from domestic fluids such as wine and spirits. It also dries very hard, which gives excellent protection against heat and finger marks. It is easy to apply with 0000 grade wire wool, and a single coat can be buffed to a hard satin finish using a soft cloth.

RUBBER OR MOUSE

French polish is best applied with a cotton cloth wrapped round a ball of cotton wool, known as a rubber, or mouse in the United States. An unwanted handkerchief makes an ideal cotton cloth. Figures 3–4 illustrate the sequence of making the rubber.

BRUSH CARE

An alternative method of applying the polish is to use a 'polishing mop'. This is a brush made of best-quality hair, usually sable or squirrel. To seal the hairs of a new mop, soak the mop in shellac (French polish) for an hour, then squeeze about half of the shellac out between your first and second fingers and lay the mop horizontally across the top of the container; leave overnight. Repeat this process for the next two days and nights. In this way, the shellac works its way into the base of the brush by capillary action, then hardens during the night, sealing the hairs into the clamp of the brush. A mop (and a brush soaked in cellulose sanding sealer) sealed in this way, will last you for years. When the bristles of a mop or brush dry hard, simply stand it in the liquid it is used for and in less than an hour it will dissolve and soften naturally. Note, however, that this will not work with pre-catalyst lacquer.

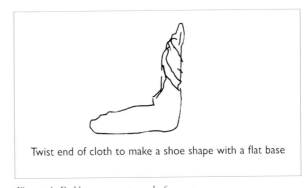

Twist end of cloth to make a shoe shape with a flat base

Figure 4: Rubber or mouse ready for use

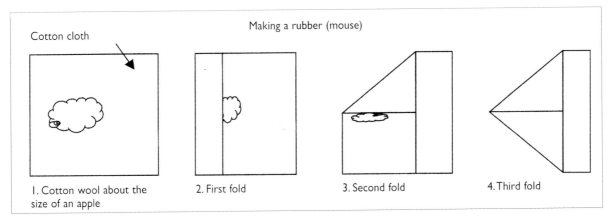

Making a rubber (mouse)

Cotton cloth

1. Cotton wool about the size of an apple

2. First fold

3. Second fold

4. Third fold

Figure 3: Order for making a polisher's rubber or mouse

NOTES ON SANDING AND FINISHING THE PROJECTS

Detailed guidelines follow for sanding and finishing each of the four furniture projects from chapter 5.

OVAL GALLERY TRAY

RECOMMENDED MATERIALS

1 coat of cellulose sanding sealer

3 coats of polyurethane satin clear varnish

Buff with Renaissance wax polish

Finishing the tray has to be carried out in three stages: first the face side of the tray, then the gallery rim (both sides) and finally the underside.

STAGE 1

The face side of the tray should have already received one coat of cellulose sanding sealer on completion of sanding, as directed earlier in this chapter. Give the tray a light sanding with 320-grit silicone carbide paper, then wipe clean with a paper towel.

Apply 3 coats of varnish, leaving four hours between coats to dry. Rub back each coat with 320-grit silicon carbide paper, using a random orbital sander after the final coat. The final coat should be rubbed back with 0000 grade wirewool.

STAGE 2

The surfaces of the gallery rim are vertical, so do not overload the brush when applying the varnish, particularly on the inside, as this could cause a build-up where the rim meets the tray base. Apply three coats sparingly to each side, rubbing back by hand, flattening the surface each

Figure 1: Stage 1, finishing the tray base

time with 320-grit silicon carbide paper, wrapped round a foam emery pad.

STAGE 3

Apply three coats, as per stage one. Finally, apply one coat of Renaissance wax polish using 0000 grade wirewool. Work with the grain when applying the wax. Buff to a hard finish with a soft cloth. The polyurethane and wax will provide the perfect durable surface necessary for an item that will certainly receive many knocks during its use.

PIER TABLE

RECOMMENDED MATERIALS

| 2 coats of shellac sanding sealer |
| Clear French polish |
| Buff with Renaissance wax polish |

A neo-classical piece of furniture such as this needs a classic finish. French polish, considered the best of all finishing materials, is the obvious choice. To avoid discolouration of the veneers used for the marquetry, it is advisable to use the 'transparent' type of French polish.

French polish is produced from a solution of shellac dissolved in alcohol. As it is applied, the alcohol evaporates leaving the shellac deposited on the wood surface. Shellac is the excreta of an insect known as *Laciffer Lacca*, a parasite found on trees in India and other eastern countries.

Apply one coat of shellac sanding sealer to the table, using either a rubber or polishing mop. When dry, lightly sand the surface with 240-grit garnet finishing paper.

Apply a second coat of sealer and again rub back with a very fine finishing paper. The sanding sealer sits on the wood, making a base foundation for the French polish that now follows.

Immerse the rubber into the French polish (or charge by squeezing the polish into the wadding) and squeeze out the surplus liquid with one hand. Dab the rubber on a sheet of white paper to remove any drips of polish. As you take the rubber to the surface, make a slanting approach from the side and keep moving across the surface, making straight-line sweeps forwards and backwards across the table surface. This is known in the trade as 'bodying up'.

Keep the rubber moving all the time. If you stop, the polish already on the surface will soften and cause a blemish. As you polish, you will feel the rubber pulling as it dries out. To leave the surface, glide the rubber smoothly off from the side of the work.

Leave the polished surface to dry, which only takes a couple of minutes. Test for dryness with the heel of your hand (not fingers). Re-charge the rubber with polish, making sure you wipe off the excess as before. This time, move the rubber in circular motions across the surface, overlapping each time. As the rubber starts to pull, smoothly remove it at one side of the table.

Repeat this process, using either circular or short figure-of-eight motions. Each time apply the polish at 90° to the direction used on the previous application. Usually 5 or 6 rubbings are sufficient; you will get a clue when the rubber starts to drag due to the dissolving action of the polish on the already hardened shellac. Leave the polish to harden for 24 hours. Place the rubber in a screw-top glass jar, adding a little methylated spirit to prevent it drying out.

The finishing stage is where a high gloss finish is obtained. The polish should this time be thinned slightly with methylated spirit. Load the rubber as before, but squeeze the rubber until almost all the polish is removed. When the rubber is dabbed on a piece of white paper, it should hardly leave a trace. Move the rubber over the surface in large figures of eight, followed by straight line motions. You should notice the edges of the polish evaporate away as the spirit dries off. Leave a few hours to harden.

Finally, the rubber should be charged with methylated spirit only and squeezed until it is almost dry. Rub over the surface in straight lines in the direction of the grain. Rub quite hard, and as the rubber dries out, you will see that it has a burnishing effect on the surface. This process is known as 'spiriting out'.

When the surface is fully hardened, a light coating of Renaissance wax polish can be applied with 0000 grade wire wool. This will produce a deep satin lustre to the surface and form a water-resistant barrier to protect against spills, as well as a hard surface to avoid finger marks.

Finish the bowed front and the table legs following the same procedures as described for the tabletop.

JEWELLERY BOX

RECOMMENDED MATERIALS

6 coats of cellulose sanding sealer
Buff with Renaissance wax polish

Before beginning the finishing process, remove all fittings from the box. Then apply one coat of cellulose sanding sealer, and rub back with 320-grit silicon carbide finishing paper. This removes the 'nibs'—the raised grain that always occurs on first coatings.

Brush on 6 more coats of sealer and leave to harden for 3 days. Sand with 320-grit silicon carbide paper. This paper removes the sealant in the form of white powder, but no clogging will occur since the paper contains an anti-clogging agent on its surface. Keep stopping to vacuum the paper and the surface to remove the powder. Look for bright spots across the surface, as these represent low areas that the paper has not reached. The number of bright spots needs to be reduced to a mere handful, before applying 0000 grade wirewool to achieve total flatness.

Finally, apply Renaissance wax polish with 0000 wire wool. Burnish with a soft cloth to achieve a very durable satin finish.

FIRE SCREEN

RECOMMENDED MATERIALS

1 coat of cellulose sanding sealer
Spray with pre-catalyst lacquer

A practical finish was needed because of the construction of the five frames with their sealed panels. The solution was to spray with cellulose-based pre-catalyst lacquer.

After sanding all parts of the wood frame and panels to achieve a smooth finish, one coat of cellulose sanding sealer is applied *to the frame only* with a standard spray gun. After drying and hardening, rub the surface back with 320-grit silicon carbide paper to remove the nibs. Note that for spraying the frame, a dedicated spray booth, along with the spray equipment, is essential. This facility may only be available to colleges and professional organizations.

Hobbyists may elect a brushed-on finish, which can be achieved very satisfactorily using the same product. Before they are mounted to the frame, the panels should be treated with one coat of cellulose sanding sealer on both sides. Remove the nibs with 320-grit silicone carbide paper. Finally, the hardened lacquer of both frame and panels should be rubbed back with 1200-grit wet or dry silicone carbide paper. The water provides the anti-clogging agent to the paper.

PROJECTS

OVAL GALLERY TRAY

D ating back to the late 18th and early 19th centuries, the gallery tray, or butler's tray as it was known in that period, forms the first of our four projects. We have chosen an oval shape as against a square or rectangular type. This design allows students to learn how to laminate veneers to build the gallery rim that surrounds the tray. This, in turn, requires making a simple jig.

CENTREPIECE

The types of decoration used in the centre of the original trays consisted of a small oval fan, shells or urns, each strangely small and disproportionate to the size of the tray. Experience has proved that either the 28-fluted oval fan or the oval patera make perfect centrepieces for this project. Both motifs complement the tray's dimensions and shape, and the designs are aesthetically and historically in harmony with the period. To complete the decoration, chevron parquetry—a 19th-century design—is added to the outside of the gallery rim.

Detailed construction of both the motifs and the parquetry is given in chapter 2. Construction of the remaining parts of the tray is given on the following pages.

TOOLS REQUIRED

Scalpel

Steel rule

Cutting board

Vacuum press or bottle jack press

Webbing clamp

Band saw or jig saw

Power sanding disc

Pillar drill

Drill bits (to match handles)

Domestic iron

Orbital palm sander

MATERIALS REQUIRED

Pommelle or a burrwood veneer (for the tray top)

Any redwood veneer (for the underside)

Laminated sepele or makoré veneer (for the gallery)

Sepele veneer (for the crossbanding)

Zebrano and dyed green veneer (for the chevrons)

Veneer (or parcel) tape, masking tape & plastic film

PVA and cascamite (now called extramite) glue

Two brass gallery tray handles

12-mm ($\frac{1}{2}$-in) thick MDF for the tray base

Assorted sheets of plywood for the jig

Hammer, nails and non-stretch string

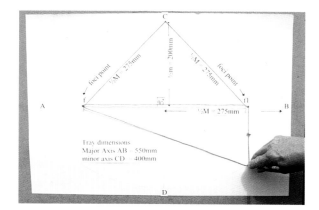

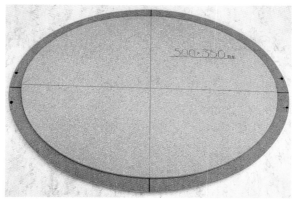

1 To produce an oval tray base from a sheet of 12 mm ($\frac{1}{2}$ in) MDF, draw a major axis (*AB*) 550 mm (22 in) long. Draw a minor axis (*CD*) 400 mm (16 in) long at 90° to *AB*, as shown. The distance from the centre to point *B* ($\frac{1}{2}$ M) is 275 mm (11 in). Pivot the rule from point *C* to a point along line *AB* that is 275 mm (11 in) from *C*. Mark this foci point *f* with a cross. Repeat on the other side of *C* making a mark *f1*. Hammer nails into *f* and *f1* and into point *C*. Tension and tie off non-stretch string around all three nails, then remove the nail at *C* and place a pencil into the loop of string and scribe an ellipse.

2 Using the same diagram as step 1, you need to produce a second ellipse 50 mm (2 in) smaller than the first. An ellipse of size 500 x 350 mm (20 x 14 in) makes an important template for later use. On both MDF boards draw two co-ordinates *xy* across the boards as shown.

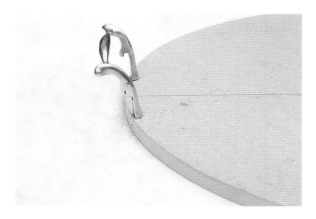

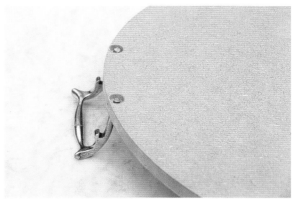

3 Measure the 'centre' between the threaded legs of the tray handles. Mark the centres on the board so that the centre *x* axis bisects the distance. Lay one of the nuts from the handle over the mark where the drilled hole is required and line up the edge of the nut with the edge of the tray base. Using a bradawl, prick a hole through the centre of the nut into the board. Drill a hole 1 mm wider than the leg of the handle. These steps ensure that the hooks on the handles fit over the gallery when it is eventually fitted. Drill all four holes in this manner.

4 Finally, turn the base over and, using a drill bit 2 mm wider than one of the nuts of the handle, drill into the previously drilled holes to make a recess about 3 mm deeper than the depth of the nut. This provides a means to conceal the nuts after the handles are eventually fitted. Precise measurements for locating the holes cannot be given because different handles will have different dimensions.

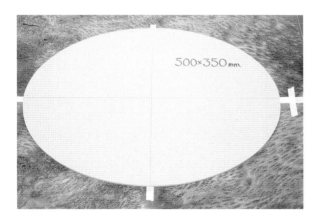

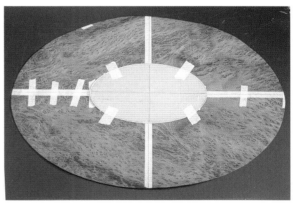

5 Lay the smaller template across the veneer chosen for the tray base. Draw round the circumference with a pencil. Also, draw the *xy* marks. Remove the template. Stick two lengths of veneer tape in line with the two *xy* marks, then draw the lines on the tape with a straight edge and pencil. The tape avoids marking the veneer. Repeat this step for the veneer that will be used for the back of the tray. Cut around the pencil marks to produce two oval background veneers for front and back.

6 The next step assumes you have constructed the centrepiece for the tray. This may be either the 28-fluted fan or the oval patera. For tuition purposes, it is assumed you have made the patera together with its surrounding stringer (see the chapter 2 section *Patera*, p. 70 for details).

Line up the patera centrally using *xy* co-ordinates as shown. Back-cut the motif into the background veneer using a scalpel. Use the edge of the stringer as a template to score the cut. (For step-by-step instructions on fitting stringing and crossbanding, see chapter 3, especially *Radius Crossbanding*, p. 100.) Insert and tape on the face side using veneer tape.

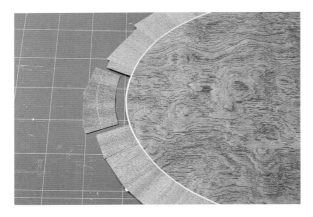

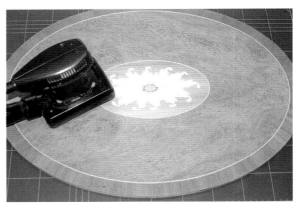

7 Fit crossbanding to the back veneer in the same manner as the front. On the back crossbanding, remove and retain the two portions that cover the two sets of recesses for the tray handles—these will be fitted after the handles are installed.

8 Glue both assemblies to both sides of the tray base at the same time to avoid cupping (bending of the MDF board). Make sure you centre the tray base to both veneer surfaces—it is important that the crossbanding sits equally around the circumference. To check this, offer the MDF base to the reverse side of the tray veneer. Line up *xy* co-ordinates and when centred, draw around the base with a pencil. Lift off the base and see if the crossbanding is of equal width all round the edge. Do the same with the back veneer. Press for 1 hour. After cleaning off the veneer tape, sand both sides and apply a finish to the front side only as detailed in chapter 4, p. 108.

9 Making the Gallery
To make the gallery rims, a simple jig is needed. Using whatever sheets of ply you have, screw sheets together to form a 50 mm (2 in) thickness. Place the tray base onto the top sheet of ply and draw round with pencil. Cut the oval out using a band saw, sawing almost up to the line.

10 Run the edge of the plywood jig around a disc sander to obtain a flat square edge of the same circumference as the tray base. Wrap plastic adhesive parcel tape around the sanded edge of the jig to prevent glue spillage from bonding the jig to the gallery rims during pressing.

11 Cut a length of 3-mm (¹/₈-in) thick hardboard, 800 x 50 mm (32 x 2 in), to make a lath. Wrap plastic adhesive parcel tape on both sides of the lath, so that when it is bent around the jig it does not snap in two. Also, the tape will prevent PVA glue sticking to the lath during pressing.

12 **Making the Laminated Rim**
Place a handle into one end of the tray (as per step 3) and measure the distance from the inside of one hook of the handle to the underside of the tray. Ours is 40 mm (just over 1¹/₂ in). This picture shows a gallery rim fitted into the hooks of the handle with the rim level with the tray base.

13 Cut 10 strips of sepele veneer, 800 x 50 mm (32 x 2 in), with the grain running along the length of the strips. Laminate 5 of the 10 strips together with PVA glue. Do this by spreading PVA glue on one strip and placing another on top, repeating for all 5 strips. A narrow wallpaper roller makes a good spreader.

14 Bend the laminated pack over the oval jig. Place the hardboard lath you made at step 11 over the laminated pack, and finally, stretch a webbing clamp around the jig, pulling the hardboard lath tight onto the laminates and the jig. Leave under pressure for 4 hours. Repeat for the other half of the rim.
We had to make the lath because our webbing clamps were only 25 mm (1 in) wide and we needed equal pressure across the whole of the 50-mm (2-in) wide rims. The hardboard lath, with its protective plastic tape, solved the problem.

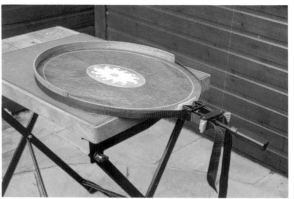

15 Make a high fence for your band saw as shown. This helps to control the rim while sawing. First trim off about 6 mm (¼ in) of the rim to form a uniform edge. Set the fence to the distance you measured the rim width to be at step 12. Run the rim through the band saw, using the high fence to keep it square to the blade. Repeat for the other rim.

16 Position one rim around one end of the tray and mark the centre of each side where the two rims are to meet and be joined with a butt joint. Cut each end of the first rim squarely. Mix a small amount of cascamite (also called extramite) and spread it on to the tray edge where the first rim is to be glued. Position the first rim over the glued side and hold in place with a webbing clamp. Wipe off any surplus glue while it is wet. Leave under pressure for 4 hours.

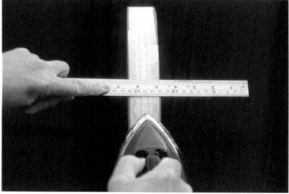

17 Repeat for the other half of the rim, but first position it with a webbing clamp (no glue) and score a line with a scalpel where the joints are to be. Saw off the surplus to both sides of the rim. Try a dry clamp again to see if the two joints are flush together without being over-tight. Glue and clamp as per the first rim.

18 Decide on the type of parquetry decoration you require for the rim. Our assembled strip consists of chevron parquetry (see chapter 2, p. 87). The strip has to be secured to the outside face of the rim, and this is best done with PVA glue and a hot iron. Position the strip around the rim so that it is centrally held with tabs of masking tape. Leave the ends overlapping at this stage. Spread PVA glue to the rim and apply heat from the iron while holding the strip in place with a steel rule. Move around the rim in this fashion. Only glue short stretches at a time.

20 Sand the outside edges of the rim and apply a finish to both surfaces of the gallery (see p. 108). Fit the tray handles, after first sawing off the surplus lengths of the bolts so that just enough of the threaded shaft is left to accept the nut without the shaft protruding above the recess.

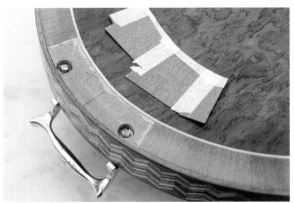

19 Do not try to force contact to every small area during your first session with the iron. Once the strip is generally in place, cut the ends to a scarf joint, as illustrated. The angled cut conceals the joint regardless of the type of decoration you apply. After the veneers have cooled down, re-apply the hot iron and press down those areas that are still proud of the rim. You will find that the second application of heat works well. There is a danger that over-exposure to heat softens the glue in the laminates of the rim. Leaving intervals to allow the work to cool down does help.

21 Finally, replace the two crossbanding pieces over both handle recesses, then glue and press with 'G' clamps. Sand the pieces level to the surrounding veneer and apply a finish to the base of the tray.

That completes the gallery tray project—just in time for that TV supper! We hope you make good use of it.

PIER TABLE

This small half-round table is our inter-pretation of an 18th-century Chippendale pier table. This classic style of furniture is a very good subject to practise both the template and fretsawing methods of marquetry.

Firstly, size and proportion must be established. It is important at this stage to take photocopies of the detailed plans that appear in the Appendix—drawings TB1 and TB2 (see pp. 168–169). The dimensions given are those used to construct Chippendale's original tables.

For the table top, you will need to draw an arc representing its full size. Using a piece of thin lath, draw the radius of the table top across a sheet of 25-mm (1-in) thick MDF. Use the lath as a trammel or beam compass by cutting a small hole or 'V' shape in one end. Hammer a panel pin or small nail into the MDF at the point that represents the radius of the circle you are going to draw. Cut out the radius using the bandsaw, smoothing the edge by sanding it on a disc sander.

TOOLS REQUIRED

Tenon saw

Gents padsaw

Combination square

Carpenter's try-square and marking gauge

Jack plane

Smoothing plane

Block plane

Flat-bottomed spokeshave

25 mm (1 in) bevelled edged chisel

18 mm ($^1/_4$ in) bevelled edged chisel

6 mm ($^1/_4$ in) bevelled edged chisel

Screwdriver

Hand or electric drill

WOODWORKING MACHINES

Rip saw

Planer/Thicknesser

Mitre (Snip) saw

Mortise machine

Spindle moulder

Bandsaw

MATERIALS REQUIRED

Hardboard

MDF

Solid timber of choice

Veneers of choice (see p. 123)

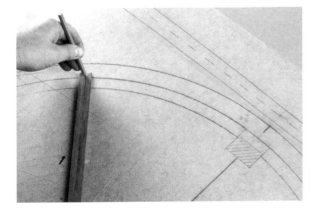

1 **Front Rail and Legs**
Mark out the position of the front rail and the legs. Do not forget to draw onto the full-size plan the position and the length of the tenons and any other jointing mechanisms you intend to use.

2 We have chosen to use MDF as the core material for the front semi circular rail because there always seem to be off-cuts around the workshop. Alternatively, as illustrated here, you can use modern bending plywood, in which the majority of laminates run the same way to assist bending.

3 Having cut out the MDF to the correct shape by making a template from the full-sized plan, it is necessary to make sure the curved rails are all the same shapes. You could do this quite successfully using a spokeshave but we have decided to machine them using the spindle moulder. A jig was made to the exact curve and each individual rail was then cut to the same shape or profile.

4 After shaping the outside edge around the spindle moulder, the inside edge received the same treatment by making a second but inward-curving jig, as illustrated.

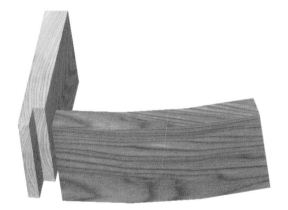

5 When they have been cut, the individual pieces can be glued together to form the complete rail. Try to stagger the joints like the joints in a brick wall; this will give the rail more strength.

6 The back rail of the table is made from solid timber to adopt strength. A simple corner lap joint is used at the corner where the back rail meets the front curved rail. Traditionally, this was often a dovetail, but unequal movement of timber results in the joint either being seen through the veneer or, worse, the veneer splitting in this area.

7 **8** Once the table legs have been cut and planed to the correct size, they need to be tapered. This again can be done by hand but, to get them all accurate, a simple jig for the circular saw can be made quite simply.

A flat piece of timber (composite material such as plywood or MDF is best) cut 150 mm (6 in) longer than the table leg and about 100 mm (4 in) wide. A tapered side is cut out so that, when the leg is fitted into the jig, it sticks out at one end by the amount of taper required and is flush at the other end. Pushing it through the circular saw in the jig produces the required taper.

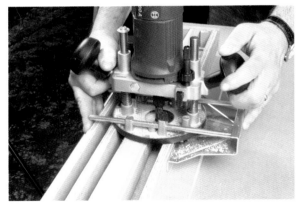

9 **10** **11** Once all the legs have been cut, plane them smooth either by hand using a smoothing plane or jack plane, or on a planing machine for quicker results. The original Chippendale table that we used as a model has mahogany tapered stringing running down each corner of the leg. To do this, another jig has to be made. It is necessary to make a box to hold the leg in place and to fit a small bridge to hold the leg level with the top of the box. Ensure that the leg fits snugly, with no movement. A small portable router is needed to run parallel with the side of the box. This produces a very clean tapered rebate for the stringing. Mahogany stringing can be bought ready-made, or you can cut your own with a circular saw. If you choose to make it yourself, make sure you have run a piece of scrap hardboard almost through the saw and secured it so as to close the saw-blade throat to a minimum, to prevent the thin stringing shattering as you cut.

Because the stringing is fitted across the top of the tapered leg as well as down the legs, a small rebate is required at this point. Using a very small saw (a fine-toothed gents saw is ideal) a spare piece of stringing can be used as a guide to run the saw against. This produces a very accurate rebate for subsequently fitting the stringing into. Once all the stringing is glued in place, plane and lightly sand to the leg surface.

12 The small spade foot to the bottom of the leg is the next detail to produce. The spade foot, traditional on this type and period of table, can be either solid or made up in four parts and applied to the surface. We have decided to make the foot using four small pieces of tapered mahogany that are mitred at the corners at 45°. This is not as difficult as you might think. Make a template out of hardwood or MDF about 150 x 50 x 12 mm (6 x 2 x $^{1}/_{2}$ in) and at one end cut an angle to match the taper of the foot. Cut a very accurate 45° mitre (through the thickness of the template) at this end. By placing the small pieces of foot (tapered to the shape of the leg) against the template and planing the edges using a block plane, the pieces will then fit around the leg, forming the spade foot. Original patterns often have a small moulded shape cut into the solid wood around the top edge, but a round shaping at this point looks very nice and is much easier.

The table top that you made earlier can be secured to the front rail. Make sure a generous overhang of approximately 25 mm (1 in) is left on the finished table. The edges of the table top need to be finished very smooth and square. On our table top a hardwood cross-grained (the grain running vertical) edge was applied to the front to assist in keeping the front edge very square, producing a crisp edge ready for veneering. There are several ways of securing the table top to the underframe. You can use modern metal or plastic brackets, but the traditional way of screwing through a pocket made in the rail is perfectly adequate.

13 The joint used to fit the leg onto the table underframe is a simple lap joint. The two back legs are corner lapped, left and right respectively, while the front leg is half-lapped into the rail. Drawing TB2 gives dimensions and views of each leg. The joints are simply cut out to the thickness of the rail, and glued and screwed. If a band saw, fitted with an accurate guide or fence, is available, you will be able to cut away the required waste (the thickness of the front rail) very easily. However, if you choose to do this by hand, mark out the waste proportion by using a try-square and a marking gauge, set to the same thickness as the front rail of the table. Cut the leg *across* the grain first, and *with* the grain for your second cut.

VENEERING AND MARQUETRY

The original pair of pier tables by Thomas Chippendale (c. 1778) were made for Denton Hall, Otley, near Leeds. They are now permanently on show at Temple Newsam House, Leeds. In deciding to make our table, we wanted to retain the veneering and marquetry designs of the originals, but a number of changes were needed for the benefit of readers who have little experience either in veneering or in marquetry. Firstly, the main background veneers used by Chippendale were satinwood and tulipwood, both very hard woods to cut and work with for beginners.

We replaced these with ripple or fiddleback maple (called tiger maple in the United States) and etimoé. Secondly, the swags of leaves on the originals were changed to swags of husks topped with ribbons, as these designs encouraged fretwork, which we wanted to include in the construction. Finally, Chippendale used penwork to highlight detailed decoration on the half-round fan and the leaves. We decided to omit this feature, not least because we have no experience in the technique. We also felt that the chosen patterns, coupled with the construction techniques, complemented the methods in this book.

TOOLS REQUIRED

Scalpel
Steel rule
Fretsaw and fretsaw table
Office stapler
Vacuum press
Cutting gauge
Pallet knife
Sponge sanding pad
Sand paper
Palm sander

MATERIALS REQUIRED

Ripple maple veneer (for the background and fan)
Magnolia veneer (for the husks and ribbons)
Sepele or etimoé (for the crossbanding)
1.5 mm boxwood stringer (dyed black)
Plain card for making the tabletop template
Half-round beading for modifying the cutting gauge
Grain filler (neutral)
Raw sienna pigment
Veneer tape and marking tape
PVA glue and paper glue

Note that for the swags and leaves, we obtained magnolia, which had violet-to-black streaks in the figuring. An alternative veneer such as black American walnut will work just as well.

All template drawings for the marquetry are given in the Appendix. The drawing of the swags for the front apron will require you to make six photocopies, and then cut and join them together in sets, as illustrated at step 18.

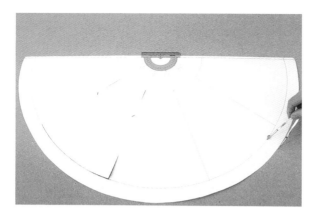

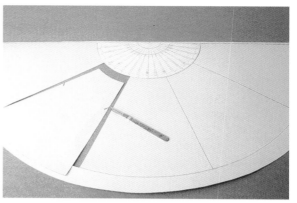

1 Cut a sheet of stiff plain card to the size and shape of the table top to form a template. First draw a 6 mm (¹/₄ in) border across the back of the template. Divide the top into five equal segments (180° divided by 5 = 36°). Use a compass to draw a curved borderline around the front of the template, 25 mm (1 in) from the front edge.

2 Centre a photocopy of the half-round fan from the Appendix up against the rear border. Using a steel rule and scalpel, cut out one of the five segments as illustrated. Retain the segment and the rest of the template for later use.

Using the half-round fan template, make a fan following the method given in chapter 2 for constructing the 28-fluted oval fan (see p. 51). Modify the number of flutes and the shape, but follow the same construction techniques.

3 The completed fan should look as above. The border around the fan consists of a dyed lovat green veneer. Alternatively, you could use magnolia, selecting a sheet that is green in colour. Keep the fan safe for later insertion into the tabletop veneers.

4 Construct a small oval fan using the template pattern given in the Appendix. Follow the same construction method given for the 28-fluted oval fan in chapter 2. The finished fan should look as above. The same green border is fitted as on the half-round fan. Retain the fan until later.

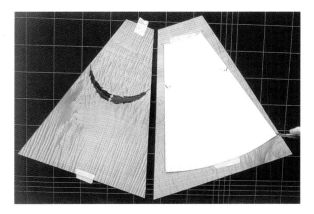

5 Using the card segment you cut out at step 2, cut five pieces of ripple maple about 12 mm (½ in) wider and 50 mm (2 in) longer than the template as shown. Make sure the direction of grain runs down the length of each segment. Place the template on top of a veneer segment. Mark and cut (with a scalpel) both sides flush to the template. After cutting three segments, make sure that the last two segments fill the area of the top before trimming them. Do this by placing the five segments edge to edge across the table top to see if they reach the back of the table. Don't cut the top and bottom edges of the segments at this stage. Make a notch cut-out 75 mm (3 in) from the top of the template on each side as shown. Mark with pencil on the veneer segments where this notch lies.

6 The two marks are used to line up the paper design after you have constructed the pad as detailed in chapter 1 (see p. 32). The five pads for fretsawing the five husk swags should each consist of the following 4 veneers: ripple maple and magnolia (or American walnut) to form the sandwich, plus any two veneers to surround the sandwich. Fretsaw each pad using a 6/0-size blade as detailed in *fretsawing* section of chapter 1 (see p. 10).

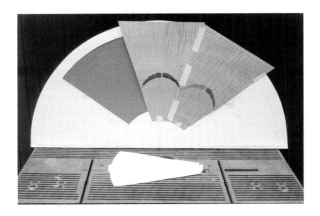

7 After fretsawing the five pads and assembling the husk swags into the ripple maple, join the segments edge-to-edge, until all five swags of husks are linked together. Place the full cardboard template centrally across the assembled five segments and cut the back edge 6 mm (¼ in) shorter to allow for the border that will run across the back edge. This will be fitted later.

8 Lay a black 1.5 mm stringer around the curved edge of the fan as described on p. 73. Leave overnight for the glue to dry fully before removing the masking tape.

9 Place the fan with its stringer centrally in line with the back edge of the top. The assembled maple and the fan should be turned over so that the taped sides are facing the cutting mat. Secure the fan to the maple with tabs of masking tape and score around the curved edge of the fan with the scalpel. Remove the fan and cut out the window following the scored cut. Insert the fan and secure with veneer tape on the taped (face) side.

10 Using the leaf template in the Appendix, place it so that it bisects the joints of the maple veneers, but touches the two adjoining swags. Draw around the template, cut out the window and the score, cut and insert all eight leaves (see step 13 below) using magnolia veneer. Cut a strip of sepele, 6 mm ($1/4$ in) wide and 790 mm (31 in) long, with the grain running along the length. Tape the strip to the back edge of the assembly with veneer tape. This forms a border to the back of the table top.

11 Tape the veneered assembly to the MDF table top, with the taped side facing you. Trim off the maple veneers that overhang the front curved edge, so that the veneers fit the shape exactly. Using a cutting gauge with the fence set to 25 mm (1 in), score a groove around the radius of the top as shown here.

Please note that a small modification is required to the cutting gauge. On one cheek of the fence, glue or pin two short lengths of half-round beading, one either side of the extension arm (see picture). These keep the fence and the cutter square to the radius edge. The fence is simply reversed when cutting against flat surfaces.

12 Mix a small amount of grain filler (neutral) with the tiniest pinch of raw sienna pigment powder. Using a pallet knife, spread and push the filler into the back of the fretsawn husks. The filler fills the tiny gaps left by the fretsaw blade, emphasizing the veins in the husks. Make sure you have first placed veneer tape across the face side of all the husks. The tape stops the filler escaping. Scrape off surplus filler with the pallet knife. Highlighting fretsawn 'accent' lines with this method is a technique that has been around since the middle of the 18th century and is still used to good effect today.

13 Cut short strips of sepele to crossband the radius edge: ten strips about 150 mm (6 in) long and 38 mm (1½ in) wide, the grain running with the *width* this time. With a length of 1.5 mm black stringing, crossband the curved edge of the assembly, at the same time trapping the stringer between the crossband and the maple segments (see chapter 3, p. 100, for step-by-step tuition). Cut a veneer to fit the underside of the table top to counterbalance the top veneer. Hinge that, and the facing assembly, to the back edge of the table-top. Spread PVA glue onto both table-top surfaces in turn, and press the whole assembly for 1 hour. Note that the grain filler is just visible across the husks.

14 Finally, cut lengths of sepele to crossband the front radius of the table. The grain must run with the 32 mm (1¼ in) width. Cut and tape strips together until they are long enough to cover the radius. Using a warm/hot domestic iron, press the crossbanding to the front edge of the table. Use a cold steel rule to follow up after the iron, to hold the veneer under pressure for a few seconds until the glue grabs. Trim away the overhanging edges with the scalpel.

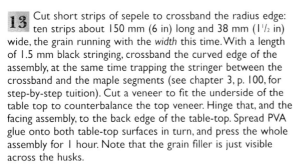

15 The top is now ready for sanding and polishing. We decided a French polish finish would best suit this classic design. Now let's decorate the apron.

16 We were invited to stand our table against Chippendale's original (one of a pair) held at Temple Newsam House, Leeds. Note the similarity in design and size. Our table had not been polished at the time this picture was taken, hence the stark contrast in colours. It was a truly great honour to have our work compared with that of England's most famous cabinetmaker.

17 The apron, or frieze, of the table consists of ripple maple as per the top, with swags of husks hanging in pairs between vertical husks. The tops of the swags are decorated with ribbons and the panel is divided in the centre with the small oval fan you made earlier. A raised crossbanding is made and glued to the bottom edge of the panel to form a border, that frames the assembly. There are six swags of husks on each side of the central fan.

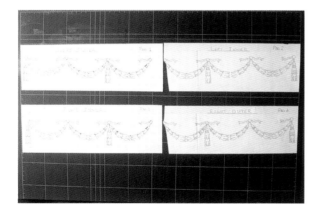

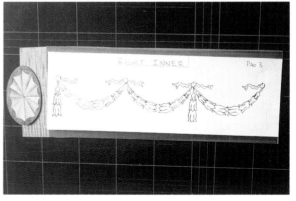

18 The four pads for fretsawing require four different patterns. Two patterns are needed for each side (left and right) of centre. The picture above shows left inner and outer (top row), and right inner and outer(below). Make up 4 fretsaw pads, each consisting of a sheet of maple and magnolia plus two wasters of your choice. Cut each veneer 330 mm (13 in) long and 95 mm (3³/₄ in) wide, the grain running with the *width*.

19 Fretsaw each pad, cutting out each husk after first sawing up the two accent lines that each husk displays. Fretsaw the ribbons, but if you are unsure about fretsawing the thin stems that link the husks to the ribbons, leave them and cut them in with the scalpel after the fretwork is assembled. Only practice improves fretwork.

20 Join up the four assembled fretworked veneers. Note that each veneer has three swags and two vertical drops of husks. You can see the joints left and right in this picture, showing the reverse side of the assembly. Cut in the central oval fan and mix a paste of grain filler and raw sienna pigment powder to fill the accent lines of the husks. You can see the stained evidence of where the paste has been applied to the left of the central fan.

21 Trim the veneer so that only 3 mm (¹⁄₈ in) overhangs each edge. This is important when using a vacuum press, since the pressure of the vacuum would damage the edge if the overhang were any greater. Apply PVA glue to the apron of the table and centre the veneer on the apron. Hold the veneer in place with about 4 tabs of veneer tape and place into the press. The plastic bag shrinks down onto the bowed shape. A strip of breather fabric (coloured grey) laid across the veneer and linked to the outlet valve ensures all air is extracted. Leave in the press for 1 hour.

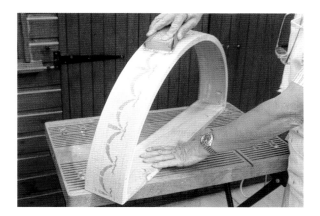

22 Trim the overhanging veneers from each side. Wet the veneer tapes and push them off with the end of a steel rule. Sand the veneer with 120-grit aluminium oxide paper, wrapped round a sponge sanding pad. The sponge pad follows the curved shape better than a cork sanding block.

23 A raised banding now has to be made and fitted around the bottom edge of the apron. The finished banding has to be three veneers thick and 12 mm (¹⁄₂ in) wide. This is achieved by first gluing and pressing together two strips of white veneers, having first made up each veneer from small lengths. The picture shows a width much wider than needed, but what is left becomes stock for later jobs. The third and final surface is made from using sepele veneer trapped between two white stringers to form the crossbanding (see steps 24 and 25).

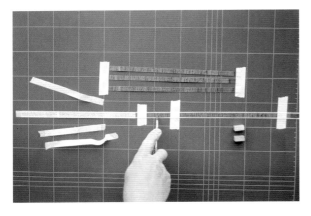

24 Cut strips of sepele 9 mm ($^3/_8$ in) wide, the grain running with the width. The three strips (top of picture) with the two 9 mm spacers (bottom right) show how the strips are cut on your marquetry cutting board. Lay a strip of 1.5 mm boxwood stringing across the cutting mat. Lay one strip of sepele crossbanding up to the stringer and place the second stringer up to the banding. Fix veneer tape across the three elements. Place a second crossbanding overlapping the first and cut through both layers with the scalpel, as shown. Avoid cutting the stringer. Remove the surplus ends and tape with veneer tape.

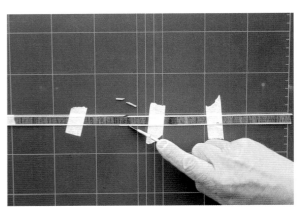

25 The stringers will have to be joined together with a scarf joint. Sit one stringer squarely on top of the other and make an angled cut as shown. The top stringer has been parted to show the angled cut. Spread PVA glue to the reverse side of the banding and stick it to the pre-prepared two-thick veneers made at step 23. Lay a steel straight edge onto the two-veneer strip to keep the glued banding straight. Hold in place with tabs of tape and press in the vacuum press for 1 hour.

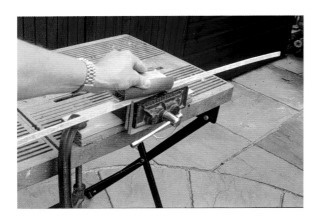

26 Cut through the two white veneers with the scalpel, using the sides of the upper crossbanding as a template. Sand the edges smooth with paper and a sanding block.

27 Spread PVA glue to the back of the assembled banding and tape it in place around the bottom edge of the apron. Place a webbing clamp around the banding and leave for 1 hour.

The finished table can be given a final light sanding and a coat of shellac sanding sealer. Finally, the table should be French polished to produce a classic finish for a classic table.

JEWELLERY BOX

One of the most popular pieces of furniture on which to display marquetry is a jewellery box. In the following project, we detail the steps to make a challenging yet achievable box, decorated with marquetry and parquetry, suitable as a gift.

The detailed plans showing dimensions and layout appear in the Appendix (see drawings JB1 & JB2). Please make photocopies of both plans before commencing the step-by-step instructions below.

The box illustrated in the following step-by-step construction is shown without an internal lining. We would recommend that you line the internal sides of the MDF base, top and walls of the box with cedar veneer, prior to construction. Also line both sides of the internal tray base. This provides a very pleasant scented aroma when the box is opened. Our box was lined after construction with solid cedar wood 3 mm ($1/8$ in) thick, but pre-veneering is perhaps an even better option.

CONSTRUCTING THE BOX

TOOLS REQUIRED

As for the pier table

MATERIALS REQUIRED

As for the pier table, plus:

12 mm ($^1/_2$ in) MDF, with the dimensions given in drawing JB1.

3-core plywood to form the base of the tray shown in drawing JB2.

Cedar of Lebanon (*Cedrus libani*) veneer, to line internal walls, base, top of box and the tray base

Mahogany hardwood strips

Two brass hinges (to the user's taste)

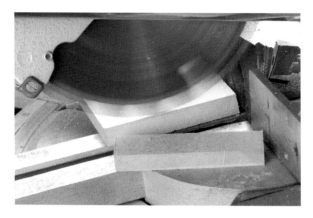

1 Use a composite material such as MDF for stability. We used a 12 mm ($^1/_2$ in) thickness for this size of box, but thinner material would be required if the box were smaller. Cut out the components accurately and remember that the angle at each end of the sides has to be 22$^1/_2$°. A compound-angle mitre saw (a snip saw) is very accurate, so long as a fence is put in place to measure each side. The 6 ends must be all the same length and the 2 centres the same. Take time to get this stage right to save time later.

2 Glue the sides to the base using PVA glue. Do not use too much glue, and wipe off any excess while it is still wet.

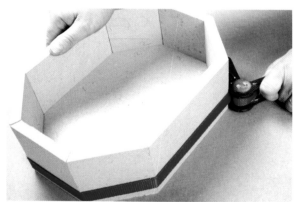

3 To hold it all together use a webbing clamp or something similar. A piece of strong cord will suffice if tightened like a tourniquet.

4 The top of the box should be cut to the exact internal dimensions of the inner sides of the box. The top has to sit halfway inside the walls of the box, so scribe a line around the edge of the top that bisects the thickness of the lid. Do this with a marking gauge. Glue and sit the top into the box to the level of the scribed line.

Box Lid

The top of the lid now forms a rebate with eight sides, each with a solid mahogany lipping cut to length, with each end angled at 22½°. The lippings are glued to the corresponding eight edges of the lid. When the assembled closed-in box is dry, plane the mahogany lippings at a 45° angle to the top to form a bevelled edge to the lid. This feature softens the appearance of the box.

Hinges

For this type of box we would recommend a good-quality hinge. Two solid drawn brass hinges, each about 25 mm (1 in) should suffice. However, if you intend to use a specialist type that incorporates a flange to stop the lid opening past 115°, then do so.

The locking mechanism is also of the maker's choice and there are various types on the market. But be aware, if a lock is to be used you may wish to make a feature of the marquetry around the escutcheon where the key fits. Also, the size of the lid may be a consideration, in limiting the size or type of lock that can be accommodated.

5 Sawing off the lid. This operation always strikes terror into the heart. However, if you have access to a band saw, accurate cutting can be achieved with the aid of a stout straight edge or guide, clamped to the saw table. Another way around this problem is to mark two parallel lines around the box where you require the lid. This is done quite simply using a mortise gauge set to about 5 mm (³/₁₆ in) and using a tenon saw to saw between the lines. Careful planing to the line, using a small block plane, achieves the necessary fit.

6 To balance the mahogany lipping fitted to the top of the box, two further lippings, made of the same wood, are required—one to the top edge of the base of the box, and another to the corresponding lower edges of the lid. This means that when the veneer is in place on the outside of the box an unsightly edge of MDF is not present. The external edges of the two lippings will have to be veneered (discussed later) but the inside edges will remain as hardwood.

INTERNAL CONSTRUCTION

The interior of the box again is an individual choice, but a jewellery box does lend itself to needing several small storage compartments. The box we have made consists of nine different compartments in the upper tray and one large compartment below. Follow the next steps to re-create the interior we have made. Remember, at this stage you may already have fitted and secured the lid with hinges. These need to be temporarily removed.

THE TRAY

The walls of the tray are made from solid mahogany,

which has been planed down to a thickness of 3 mm ($^1/_8$ in). The base of the tray consists of two cedar veneers glued either side of a sheet of 3-core plywood. The base should be cut to size and the two cedar veneers glued, pressed and sanded before the walls of the two trays are attached.

The upper tray needs to be shallow for easy access. Drawing JB2 shows an octagonal tray with eight compartments surrounding an integral, yet smaller octagonal tray. The two trays have to be constructed separately, before fitting the eight dividing walls which form the eight outer compartments.

7 The integral tray is made exactly like the main tray, but this will be explained later. When cutting the sides of the tray, great care must be taken to ensure that you have cut them to exactly the right length, which includes the angle at each end. Number them so that they will correspond to the sides of the tray base.

8 Once all of the sides have been cut and checked for accuracy of fit, they can be glued in place around the tray base. Do not use too much glue at this stage. Cleaning off excess glue inside a confined space is very difficult. To clamp the eight sides to the tray base, you will need either a webbing clamp or a piece of strong cord to use as a tourniquet.

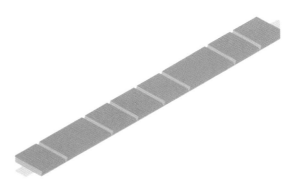

9 The next stage is to build the integral tray. Draw a line around the inside of the tray base that corresponds to where you want the inner tray. Use a small piece of wood as a guide that will help to keep an accurate distance all around. The central compartment needs to be smaller in height than the outside edge of the tray. Cut the eight sides to the measurements given on the plan drawing, remembering that each end must be cut at an angle of $22\frac{1}{2}°$.

10 The eight sides of the central tray should be laid out flat on a length of masking tape so that the ends touch each other. Place a small amount of PVA glue in each joint, then bring the tape around into a circle and the box will automatically form the correct shape. Place a piece of strong cord around the box and tighten with the tourniquet method (the sticky tape can be removed when the glue sets).

At this stage, check that the integral tray you have just made is the same shape as the outline you have drawn on the inside of the tray base. Also remember to use the integral tray as a template to draw the profile onto the timber you have chosen to make the small lid. Do this before gluing the tray in place.

MAKING THE EIGHT DIVISIONS

The next stage is to make the divisions that connect the integral tray to the outer walls of the main tray. If they are shaped like the ones in our box, not only do they look correct but they help to draw the eye in to the centre of the box.

To make the joints at the points where the divisions meet the two trays, two different cuts are required. At the outer end, where the division meets the outer wall, a bevelled point is required, whereas at the other end, where the division meets the integral tray wall, a bird's beak cut is required. In both cases a small chisel will perform the cuts. Each division will need to be fitted and glued individually. Make sure when you are fitting the divisions that they are put in place square and plumb. Use a small offcut of wood, cut square with great care, to use as a guide.

The top edges of the divisions will need a slightly rounded profile. This should be done after they are glued in place, using an abrasive paper. Steps 11 and 12 illustrate the divisions.

11

12

13 The integral tray lid can be made from any material of your choice. You must decide at this stage whether you are going to veneer the top of the lid or use a solid decorative timber. Whatever your choice, carefully plane the edges, using a block plane, until the lid is exactly the same size as the central compartment. Then cut a rebate to help position the lid.

14 If using solid timber for the centre tray lid, plane the top into a slight cushion shape to enhance its look. To do this, pencil a parallel line around the top edge, 18 mm (^{3}/$_4$ in) from the edge. Then mark another line on the edge of the lid 5 mm (^{3}/$_{16}$ in) down from the top edge. Simply plane between the lines making a slight cushion shape. Follow the three pictures shown below.

Finishing The finished tray needs four legs to stand on, when placed in the box. Using a piece of hardwood, 6 mm (^{1}/$_4$ in) square and about 100 mm (4 in) long, shape it with a block plane so that two adjacent sides form a 22^1/$_2$° angle. Round over the other corner with some abrasive paper. Cut the wood into lengths of 18 mm (^{3}/$_4$ in). Glue them to the four angles where the front and back panels meet their adjacent smaller panels. Hold with masking tape until the glue sets. This allows the tray to stand over the lower single compartment.

The next task is to make the small half-round moulding at the bottom edge of the box. This is just a small piece of hardwood (the same as the type used for the bevelled detail on the top). This strip of wood is 3 mm (^{1}/$_8$ in) square and long enough to go all around the box. Again using the block plane and holding one end of the strip of wood flat on the bench, plane it to a 'D' shape, Take care to have only a very small amount of blade protruding from the plane base. Finish off with fine abrasive paper, taking care not to abrade the back edges that will be glued to the box. Cut the moulding to the correct length of each side (including the mitres), then mitre at the corners and glue in place. Use masking tape to hold them in position while the glue dries.

VENEERING AND DECORATING THE BOX

Veneering a box that includes both marquetry and parquetry requires a degree of planning and thought. It is always advisable to decide first on the colours of woods you want to use, and which woods work best with the shape of the item.

We decided at the outset that the lid of the box would hold a single white rose—the emblem of our beautiful county of Yorkshire, which we are both passionately proud of. It also offered an opportunity to teach readers how to construct a rose using the window method.

The beadings and bevelled edges around the base and lid respectively are made of mahogany. To contrast with the mahogony, we decided to use burr ash and burr yew as the two main veneers. The burr yew is set in panels with quartered corners. This type of corner adds a regency appearance to the piece, and the surrounding burr ash offers a clean contrast, making the panels stand out. To separate the panels from the borders, a 1 mm black stringing line is cut-in around each panel. The burr yew proved quite a challenge because the knots kept dropping out, needing regular replacement. The effort and frustration was, however, worthwhile in the end. Many woods present these problems, but burrs are always easier to repair *in situ* and, because of their random pattern, the repair is always totally invisible.

To complete the box, the eight panels forming the edge of the lid were covered with chevron parquetry. This project is challenging, yet achievable for students or hobbyists with a minimum of experience in marquetry and veneering. You may wish to change the choice of veneers for your box, but regardless of choice, the method of construction remains the same.

TOOLS REQUIRED

Scalpel
Steel rule
Selection of 'G' clamps
Gents padsaw
Tenon saw
Mitre box
Vacuum press
Compass and pencil
Cutting gauge
£1 coin (or another coin of 22 mm / ⅞ in diameter

MATERIALS REQUIRED

(veneers are as used by us; others can be substituted)
Makore, ash burr, yew burr and black dyed sycamore
Poplar and sycamore (for the white rose)
1.5 mm black stringing
Plain white card
Veneer tape
Masking tape
PVA glue
Plastic adhesive film

1 First, make up templates from plain white card: one for each of the eight panels on the lower half of the box and one for the lid. For the lid, cut the card so that it fits the surface of the lid perfectly. Tape it in place and, using a compass or a cutting gauge, scribe a line about 25 mm (1 in) from all eight sides. Using a scalpel and rule, cut out the inner octagonal shape.

2 For each of the eight lower panels, cut the card so that it covers a panelled area completely. Measure a border from each of the four sides of the card at about 9 mm ($^3/_8$ in). Join up the four sides using a pencil and rule. Take a £1 coin (or another coin about 22 mm [$^7/_8$ in] diameter) and line it up at each corner to two pre-measured marks 10 mm ($^3/_8$ in) either side of a corner and scribe around the coin to form the quartered corner. Repeat on each panel in this fashion. Cut out each inner panel with scalpel and rule.

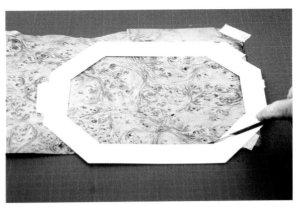

3 Lay the outer template for the lid across the burr yew and secure with masking tape. Using the template as a guide, cut around the inner sides of the card to produce the central panel for the lid.

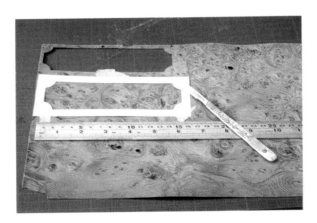

4 For each of the eight templates for the side panels, lay them in turn across the burr yew and cut around the inner sides of the cards to produce the panels. You would be advised to number the panels and mark corresponding numbers on the box sides.

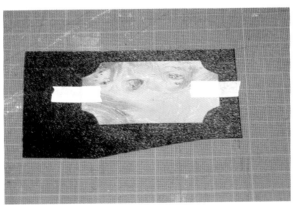

5 With a sheet of black-dyed veneer, lay one burr yew panel across a sheet of black, so that the grain of the black veneer is running with the length of the panel. Secure them together with two tabs of masking tape. Score around the side of the panel where the yew meets the black veneer. Remove the yew veneer and cut out the black, following the scored line. Fit the yew panel back into the window of the black veneer and rub PVA glue into the joints. Repeat for the other 7 panels. Leave the glue to set and cure for a minimum of two hours before working further on them.

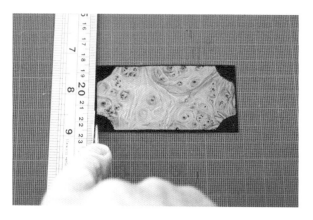

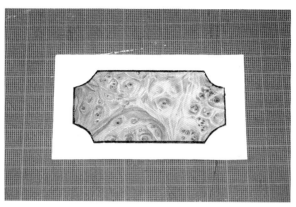

6 Once the PVA has fully dried, you need to cut the black veneer so that only a 1-mm wide stringer remains around the panel. For the four straight sides, you can carefully line up the rule along the black veneer, judging a 1 mm distance from the panel as you do this. Cut along the rule to remove the surplus black veneer. The quartered corners will have to be cut freehand. You will soon get the hang of cutting on the same imaginary line around the panel. Even though you are cutting across short grain for the two ends and the four corners, the PVA glue should hold the 'stringers' in place.

7 After completing all eight panels, lay one of them on top of a sheet of ash burr. Secure with tabs of masking tape, then score around the joint where the two veneers meet. Remove the panel and cut out the ash burr window. Insert and glue the yew panel in place. Proceed to step 8 before inserting the remaining seven panels.

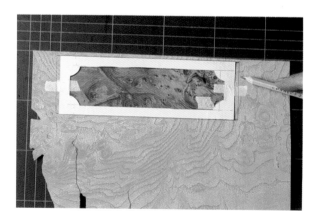

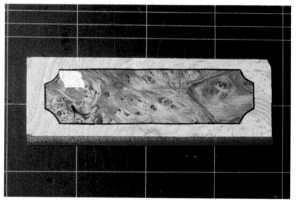

8 Using each side template in turn, lay them over the assembled yew and ash bordered panels so that the window of the template fits centrally over the yew panel. Cut along the top and bottom edges using the template as the guide. Make the width of the panel 3 mm ($^1/_8$ in) wider than the template at each side. This is to allow for sanding to the box shape after gluing each panel in place.

9 Cut eight strips of makoré or sepele veneer 6 mm ($^1/_4$ in) high and the length of each panel. These need to be secured to the top edge of each panel with veneer tape to the face side. Repeat steps 7 to 9 for the other seven panels. Place the eight completed panels under a weight to keep them flat while you complete the remaining jobs.

10 To build the white rose, go to chapter 2, p. 62, for step-by-step tuition. After completing the rose and installing it into the burr yew panel, it is ready to be glued to the lid of the box. Centre the octagonal veneer across the lid, taking careful measurements to get it as near central to the eight sides as possible. Tape the top edge to the lid with veneer tape to form a hinge. Draw around the eight sides of the veneer with pencil and lift the veneer to expose the area to be glued.

11 Spread PVA glue thinly but evenly across the area of the lid contained within the pencil lines. Use a 25 mm (1 in) wallpaper roller to spread the glue. Flip the assembled panel back across the glue and press for ten minutes only. Our two-part pressing technique allows you to centre the panel on the lid using the cutting gauge. This ensures that borders and stringers, when fitted, mitre correctly at all eight corners.

12 Using a cutting gauge set at a width of about 28 mm (1 1/8 in), test that the gauge will remove a tiny strip off each side of the octagonal panel. Remember that you set the border width at 25 mm (1 in) when you made the template, so if you have aligned the panel as accurately as possible onto the lid, you should be taking just enough from each side. In this way, the panel is now centred on the lid between all eight sides. Remove the surplus veneers with a sharp chisel or scalpel and return the lid to the press for one hour.

13 Measure and cut eight strips of ash burr to form the borders for the panel of the lid. Make sure enough length exists to form an overlap at each mitre. Cut eight lengths of 1.5 mm black stringing, one for each of the eight sides. The stringers reside between the panel and the eight borders.

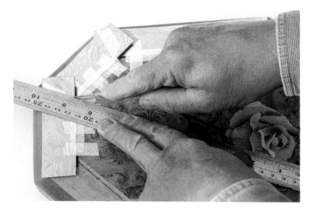

14 Make sure veneer tape is placed along the area where the mitres are to be cut. Tape both the upper and lower veneer. Place the steel rule in line with the points where the stringers cross, and the outer edges where the borders cross. Pressing hard and without moving the rule, cut through both veneers and both stringers to form the mitre. Complete all mitres in this manner.

15 Finally, flip back two opposing sides in turn and run PVA glue onto the lid surface. Glue all borders and place in the press for one hour.

16 Glue the eight panels to the bottom half of the box, two at a time. Do this by spreading PVA glue to one panel of the box. Offer a veneered panel to the glue, making sure it sits squarely on the beading protruding at the foot of the panel and that the overhang is equal on both sides. Place a few layers of protective paper and prepared strips of MDF or ply to both the inside and outside of the box and fix 'G' clamps, pressing for one hour. Sand the two ends flush with the angle of the box, making sure you sand towards the edge and not into it—otherwise it will break. Complete the other six panels in pairs in this fashion.

17 Chevron parquetry: see chapter 2 (p. 90) for tuition on building this design. Once all eight chevron panels have been constructed they should be glued to the side panels of the box lid, following the procedure in step 16. That completes the marquetry and parquetry work.

For directions on sanding and finishing, see chapter 4.

FIRE SCREEN

Although the fire screen is a piece of furniture not often found in modern houses, it is nevertheless something that gives the furniture maker and the marqueteur an excellent subject on which to practise their craft.

There are many different styles of fire screen but this one is very well designed and allows the marqueteur plenty of scope to design rural scenes or totally abstract patterns. There is no reason why this style of screen should not lend itself to being made large enough to be used as a dressing screen if desired.

CONSTRUCTION DIMENSIONS

Copy the plans given in the Appendix. Drawings SC1 and SC2 show detailed dimensions, while SC2 also shows an exploded view of one frame.

In creating the curve on the top rail of the screen, it is particularly important to draw the plan to full size. The detailed plan (SC1) gives the two radii from which the top curve can be made, using a trammel beam as a compass.

If you take your time and draw this very important stage well, the drawing will also act as a setting-out plan (or rod, as it is called).

All the screen components must be accurately sized and machined, ready for the joint work to be started. All the positions of the joints and the lengths of the components can be marked off from the dimensions given on the plans. The shape of the top rails will have to be transferred from the full-size drawing to the timber, using a tracing on tracing paper.

Our choice of timber for the fire screen was cherry. This is a very clean timber with attractive grain and is not too expensive to buy at your local timber supplier. The advantage of using cherry for this project is that the frame will not dominate the screen; therefore, the marquetry will be shown off to its maximum effect.

The size of the screen legs and rails is quite adequate for a screen of this size, because it is important not to have the frame so heavy that it dwarfs the panels and takes the emphasis off the marquetry. Overall proportion is, of course, very important. Most furniture is taller than it is wide and therefore looks correct. This would be correct for a fire screen if it did not, as this does, fold in a concertina fashion. Because of this mechanism, the screen would look out of proportion if it were flat, but because it will always be standing in a concertina configuration, its proportions are correct. The curved rail softens the design.

TOOLS REQUIRED

As listed for the pier table, plus:

Round-bottomed spokeshave

Fore plane

Portable router

Soss/zysa hinges

MATERIALS REQUIRED

As listed for the pier table, plus:

Cellulose sanding sealer

Cellulose lacquer

1 Each panel is held in the frame by a groove running all around the inside. Each panel is made from 6 mm ($^1/_4$ in) MDF and veneered with standard-thickness veneers. The panels, when complete with the veneers, must be sanded prior to inserting them into the frame.

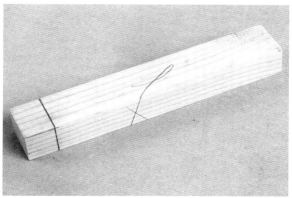

2 Once the sizes of your rails have been established by marking off the length, plus the tenon length at each end, you need to choose the face side and mark it accordingly. Mark out the mortises and tenons to the dimensions given in drawing SC2. Ideally, a mortise should correspond to a chisel size.

3 Cutting the mortises can be done either by machine or by hand, whichever you prefer. Remember that you will need to haunch the tenons for both the depth of the groove and also the other side of the tenon to stop the mortise being exposed. If cut by hand then they must be done carefully with a tenon saw. However, a simple alternative is to make a jig and use a portable router with at least a 12 mm ($^1/_2$ in) straight cutter (see next illustration).

4 The router jig can also be used to cut the tenons with angled shoulders, but it is often better to cut the shoulders with a tenon saw first; the router can then be traversed back and forth to remove the waste material. Approaching the task in this way alleviates the problem of grain splitting when, inevitably, going against the grain on one side of the rail.

5 Notice the two wedges, laid head-to-tail to each other, at the far end of the jig. These make sure the timbers are held tight during routing, to prevent any movement and possible accident or damage to you or the timbers.

6 The groove in the rails can be cut using a hand plough plane, a small portable router or spindle moulder. Whichever apparatus you have, the width of the groove must match the thickness of the panel so the panel is held firm, but not too tight. Remember that the panels must be sanded prior to fitting in the frame, and if possible a coat of sealer applied. The depth of the groove in this instance should be 10 mm (^{3}/$_8$ in). When using solid timbers, slight movement of the timber is quite probable. Coating the panel with sealer will help to prevent a visible line appearing as the frame starts very slightly to shrink.

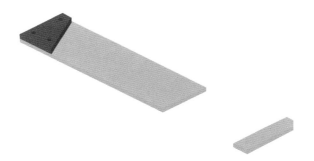

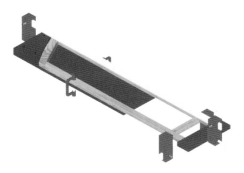

7 Make a simple jig (as illustrated) to enable you to clamp the screens together. The jig is shaped to the angle of the top rail, with the top edge parallel to the bottom rail when in use. The angle of the top rail changes slightly with each panel, so the angle of the jig needs adjusting to suit. The profiled rail is fastened to a flat MDF or plywood board the width of one screen.

8 Practise assembling the frame without glue to make sure all the parts fit together, then take it apart and re-assemble using glue. Only the mortises and tenons require a thin coat of glue; the panels rely solely on the groove to keep them in place. A sash clamp and the jig made at the previous step allow the frame to be glued and clamped together. Two 'G' clamps prevent the frame slipping from the jig as the sash clamp is tightened. For illustration purposes the marquetry panels are not shown here, but clearly you will have inserted them prior to assembly.

9 Once the glue has dried, the shaping of the top rail can begin. The most straightforward way to achieve this is by using a flat-bottomed and a round-bottomed spokeshave, working with the grain. The profile shape of the top rail needs to be semi-circular at the top. Draw a line parallel to the top, 8 mm ($^5/_{16}$ in) down from the top edge at both sides, and another line on the top of the rail, lengthways in the middle. These lines will act as a guide when you spokeshave the profile. Once you have adopted a satisfactory profile, abrasive paper should be used to smooth the finished shape.

Fitting the individual sections together is a task done with a large plane, such as a fore plane or a jack plane. The edges should fit snugly together with no gaps, ready for fitting the hinges.

10 The specialist hinges used for the screen are called either soss or zysa hinges, and conveniently fit directly into the edge of each panel. Make sure that when fitting the hinges, accurate marking-out is achieved by using a craft knife, or utility knife, to mark out the positions in pairs. Drill the appropriate size of hole, both for the barrel of the hinge and the depth, as instructed by the manufacturer.

As a finish, the panels were first sealed on both sides with two coats of cellulose sanding sealer, prior to installing them in their respective frames. Finally, the frames and panels were sprayed with cellulose lacquer to give a satin finish.

THE MARQUETRY DESIGN

Members of the Leeds Marquetry Group constructed the marquetry shown on the two sides of the screen. It took approximately four months to complete with members of all ages and skill-levels taking part, including a fourteen-year-old junior.

Two themes were selected; one Oriental, representing koi carp and butterflies with bamboo plants, and the other heralding the first flush of an English spring, showing spring flowers, rolling hills and the arrival of swallows. A group member and artist Elizabeth Dorree drew the designs to scale and purposefully chose vibrant colours to encourage the use of many dyed woods. All the panels have bird's-eye maple as the main background veneer, which complements the cherry frame. Using Elizabeth's line drawings, each member cut his or her chosen marquetry into either a veneer or cardboard waster. On completion, the work was back-cut into the maple, using the reverse window method.

Should you wish to make this item of furniture, we think it would probably be done with a specific purpose in mind and therefore you would want to design your own decoration. Because of this, we do not intend to illustrate how the Leeds design was put together. Suffice it to say that the project gave the group members great fun and satisfaction, working together towards a common goal. We are very grateful for their support, skill and achievement, which this highly imaginative and unique piece of furniture represents.

CHAPTER SIX
FURNITURE MAKERS' GALLERY

FIRE SCREEN
MADE BY JOHN APPS AND THE LEEDS MARQUETRY GROUP

We took the bold decision from the outset to involve as many people as possible in its construction. John's stylish frame provides the perfect surround to complement a marquetry theme. Members of the Leeds Marquetry Group each contributed to the ten panels which make up the two-sided screen. Artist and group member Elizabeth Dorree created the line drawings to scale for each panel. Dyed veneers were used wherever possible—a bold, but correct, decision.

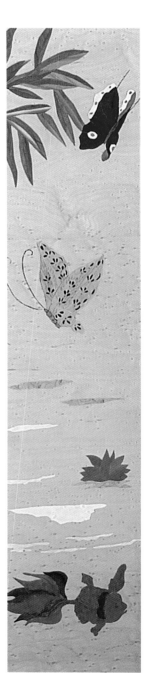

Fire screen – side 1: An Oriental garden

Fire screen – side 2: An English garden and the first arrival of swallows

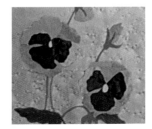   

ORIENTAL VASE
MADE BY FRED DAY (1877–1955)

This amazing example of woodcraft was donated to the Abbey House Museum, Kirkstall, Leeds in late 2002 by the family of the late Fred Day of Armley, Leeds. Taking nine years to complete, the vase, standing 380 mm (15 in) high encompasses marquetry, parquetry, laminating, woodcarving, woodturning, and working in miniature form. The cabriole legs, dragons and shoulders on the corners are all built from solid wood laminations, each consisting of extraordinary parquetry arrangements. The four miniature marquetry scenes suggest construction by the window method, despite the fact that the piece was made before 1930—some twenty-five years before the method is first recorded as being used. A lion's whiskers and a spider's web, when examined under the microscope, show that fine-line slivers of wood were inserted into the miniaturized pictures with precision cutting.

Each foot, less than 25 mm (1 in) in diameter, consists of over 220 section of wood with the patterns running to the centre of the wooden balls. One ball was broken, showing evidence of the laminations inside.

Oriental vase lion panel

Oriental vase peacock panel

Oriental vase spider's web panel

Oriental vase church panel

OCTAGONAL PEDESTAL TABLE
MADE BY JACK METCALFE

The segmented flutes were constructed by the template method, using a modified circle cutter to fit the large radius. Each flute comprises alternating segments of oak and oak burr, separated from adjacent flutes by a boxwood stringer. The attractive shape and size—880 mm (34¹/₂ in) in diameter—make this the perfect breakfast table.

LION IN CAGE
MADE BY FRED DAY (1877–1955)

Carved from one block of wood, measuring only 50 x 75 x 75 mm (2 x 3 x 3 in), the 'lion in a cage' sits on a chassis with a turning axle supported by four revolving wheels and a cage door that swings open. Every aspect of Fred Day's miniature carving remains captive to the wood it originated from.

Octagonal pedestal table

Lion in cage also displayed in Leeds museum

ITALIAN DRINKS TROLLEY
MADE BY JACK METCALFE

An Italian-made trolley, veneered in 1996 and decorated with marquetry set into book-matched black American walnut burr.

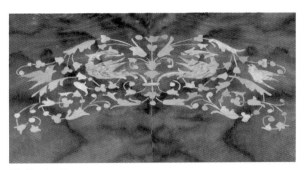

Trolley with side down

Trolley detail

SOFA TABLE
TOMOKO HASUO, FORMER STUDENT OF LEEDS COLLEGE OF ART AND DESIGN AND LEEDS MARQUETRY GROUP

Made by a marquetry student, the table demonstrates Tomoko's marquetry and cabinetmaking skills as well as her attention to detail. Each leaf of the elegant underframe is hand carved and jointed into the uprights. Having completed her course, Tomoko has gained employment in York with a highly respected furniture maker.

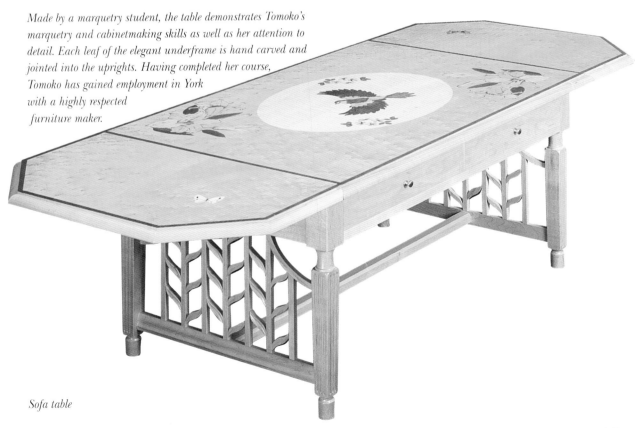

Sofa table

SEWING BOX
MADE BY ALAN ROLLINSON

The standard of marquetry and parquetry shown here belies the short time Allan had been studying it. Alan's affinity with marquetry continues, as he commences a two-year course at York College.

Sewing box closed

Sewing box open

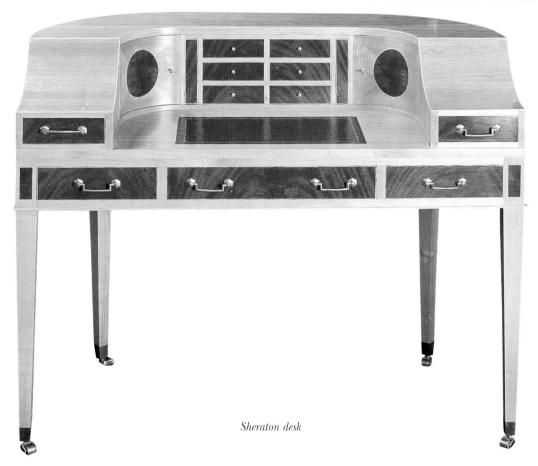

Sheraton desk

CARLTON HOUSE DESK
MADE BY JOHN APPS

The semi-circular back is cast in one piece by laminating several sheets of 1.5 mm areo ply around a profiled former. Traditional mortise and tenon joints are used where the curved and front rails meet. The drawer construction was traditionally made using cedar linings and the dovetails were cut by hand. The solid timber and most of the veneer was French cherry, as the desk was to look as near as possible to satinwood, a timber very difficult to obtain in the sizes required. Decoration was achieved with matched mahogany curl to provide a very impressive contrast. A vacuum press was used to secure the veneers to the curved surfaces. A specialist locksmith solved the problem of providing security fittings to the two curved doors, which had to meet the front faces at an angle of 12°. The second picture reveals one of the two secret compartments that emerge after releasing the locking mechanism inside the curved door.

Sheraton desk secret compartments

Anthemion box

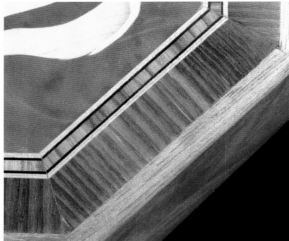

Anthemion box detail

ANTHEMION BOX
MADE BY JACK METCALFE

An Italian-made box decorated with the anthemion (honeysuckle) design much evident in the neo-classical period, both in Robert Adam's plaster casts and in Chippendale's furniture. Note the blue border veneer—a product of injecting a beech tree, as discussed in Chapter 1: Materials.

PARQUETRY GALLERY TRAY
MADE BY TONY THORPE

An impressive and eye-catching parquetry design, off-set with traditional corner fans, makes this work unique. Note the pattern repeated around the gallery rim. Tony won the John Boddy Trophy for the best applied entry in the group 2001 Seaton Cup competition.

Parquetry gallery tray

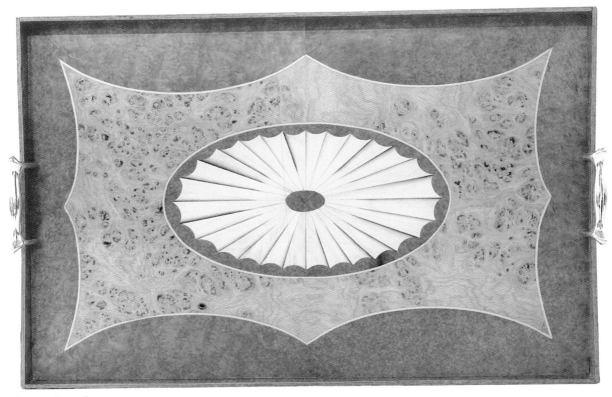

Rectangular gallery tray

RECTANGULAR GALLERY TRAY
MADE BY JENNY GROUT

Jenny made this tray for her Duke of Edinburgh bronze award scheme when she was just 15, during her year's stay with the Leeds Marquetry Group. This was her first marquetry work. The scalloped panel of oak burr complements the oval fan and demonstrates her creative qualities.

CHINESE FIRE SCREEN
MADE BY MARGARET CAPITANO

The Chinese lady provides a fitting picture for this simple yet colourful fire screen. A hinged stay bracket at the back keeps the screen upright. Margaret, a tailoress by trade, selected the woods for the clothing and matching ensemble, making a delightful composition.

Chinese fire screen

LONG CASE CLOCK
MADE BY CHARLES KERR

This delightfully decorated clock demonstrates both marquetry and cabinetmaking skills, and took first prize at the 2002 Axminster Show.

GREAT WALL OF CHINA SCREEN
MADE BY JACK METCALFE

A beech hardwood frame with decorative inlayed banding and a sculptured top surrounds a marquetry picture of China's Great Wall. The pale morning sky is well represented by lemon wood.

Great Wall of China screen

Long case clock

Appendix

TEMPLATES FOR DESIGNS IN CHAPTER TWO

Rose, Shell and Concave Corner Fan

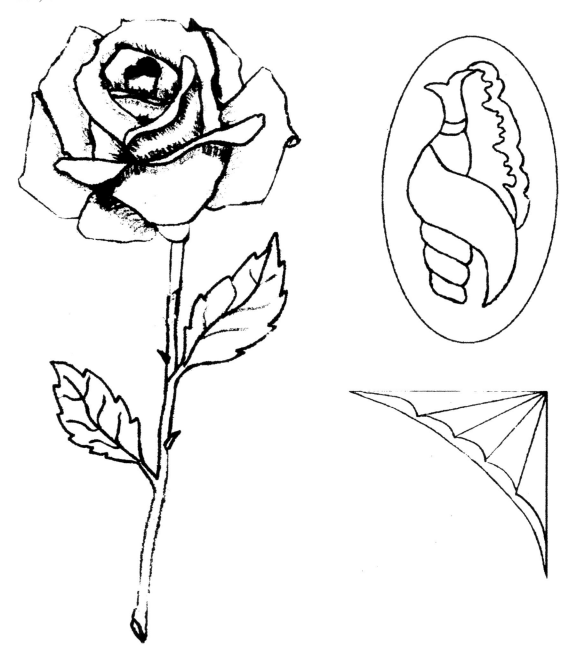

TEMPLATES FOR OVAL FAN

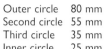

COMPASS ROSE

Outer circle 80 mm
Second circle 55 mm
Third circle 35 mm
Inner circle 25 mm

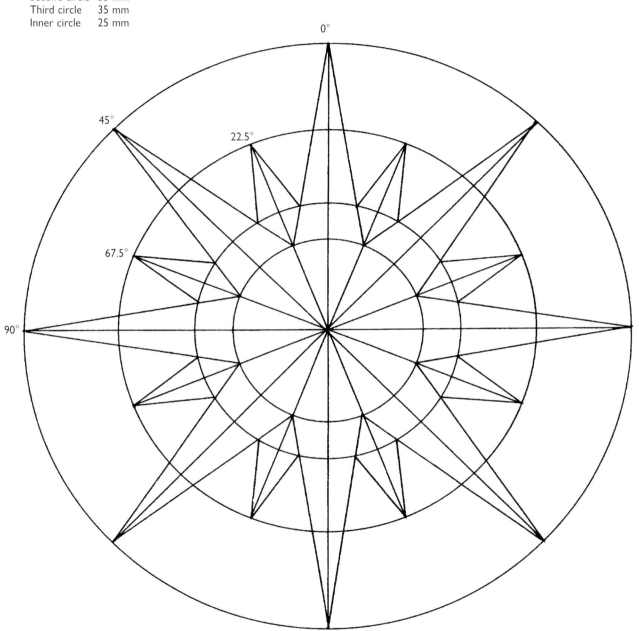

PATERA

HALF-ROUND FAN

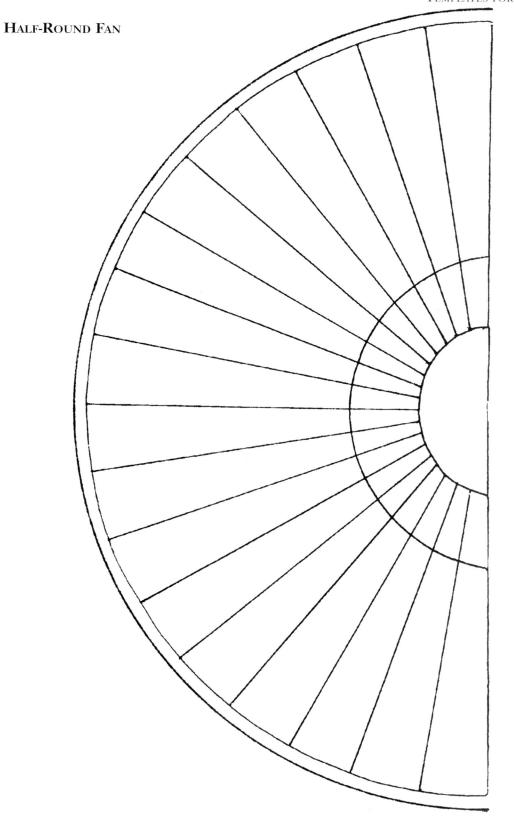

PIER TABLE TEMPLATES

VENEER PRESS

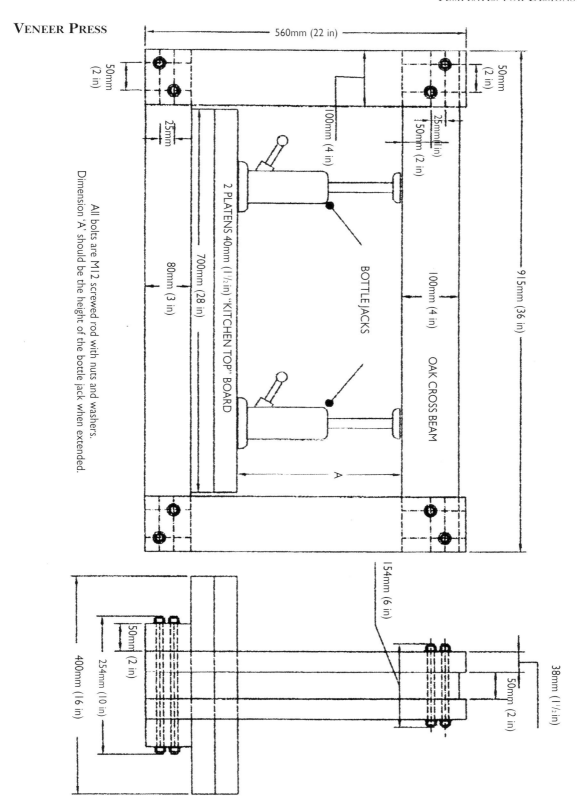

560mm (22 in)

50mm (2 in)

50mm (2 in)

25mm

100mm (4 in)

25mm (1 in)

50mm (2 in)

915mm (36 in)

2 PLATENS 40mm (1½ in) "KITCHEN TOP" BOARD

80mm (3 in)

700mm (28 in)

BOTTLE JACKS

100mm (4 in)

OAK CROSS BEAM

A

All bolts are M12 screwed rod with nuts and washers.
Dimension 'A' should be the height of the bottle jack when extended.

154mm (6 in)

50mm (2 in)

254mm (10 in)

400mm (16 in)

38mm (1½ in)

50mm (2 in)

DRAWINGS FOR PROJECTS IN CHAPTER FIVE

PIER TABLE (TB1)

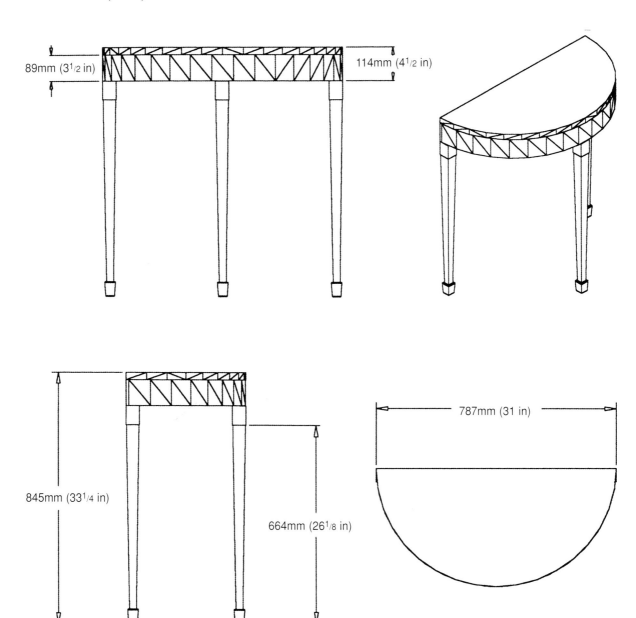

PIER TABLE (TB2)

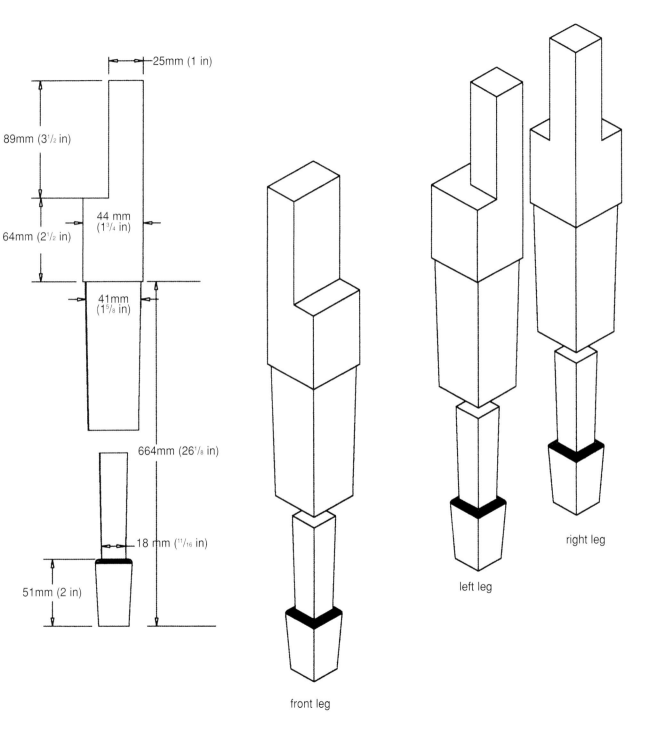

25mm (1 in)

89mm (3¹/₂ in)

44 mm (1³/₄ in)

64mm (2¹/₂ in)

41mm (1⁵/₈ in)

664mm (26¹/₈ in)

18 mm (¹¹/₁₆ in)

51mm (2 in)

front leg

left leg

right leg

JEWELLERY BOX (JB1)

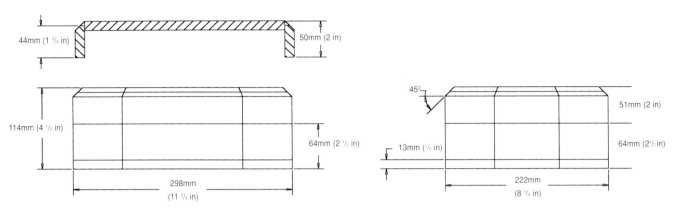

44mm (1 ³/₄ in)

50mm (2 in)

114mm (4 ¹/₂ in)

64mm (2 ¹/₂ in)

298mm
(11 ³/₄ in)

45°

51mm (2 in)

13mm (¹/₂ in)

64mm (2¹/₂ in)

222mm
(8 ³/₄ in)

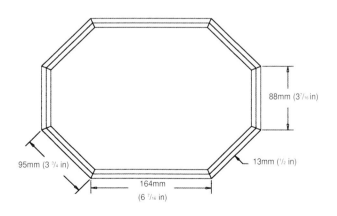

88mm (3⁷/₁₆ in)

95mm (3 ³/₄ in)

13mm (¹/₂ in)

164mm
(6 ⁷/₁₆ in)

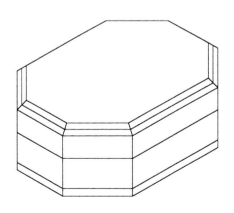

JEWELLERY BOX
(JB2)

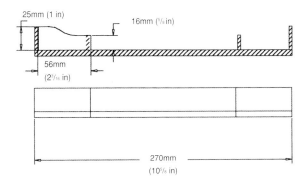

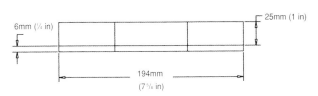

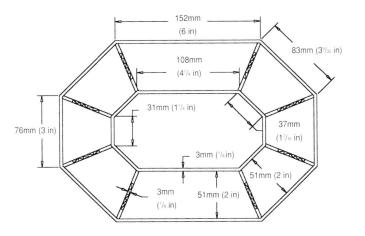

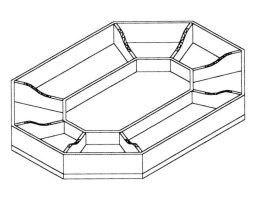

FIRE SCREEN (SC1)

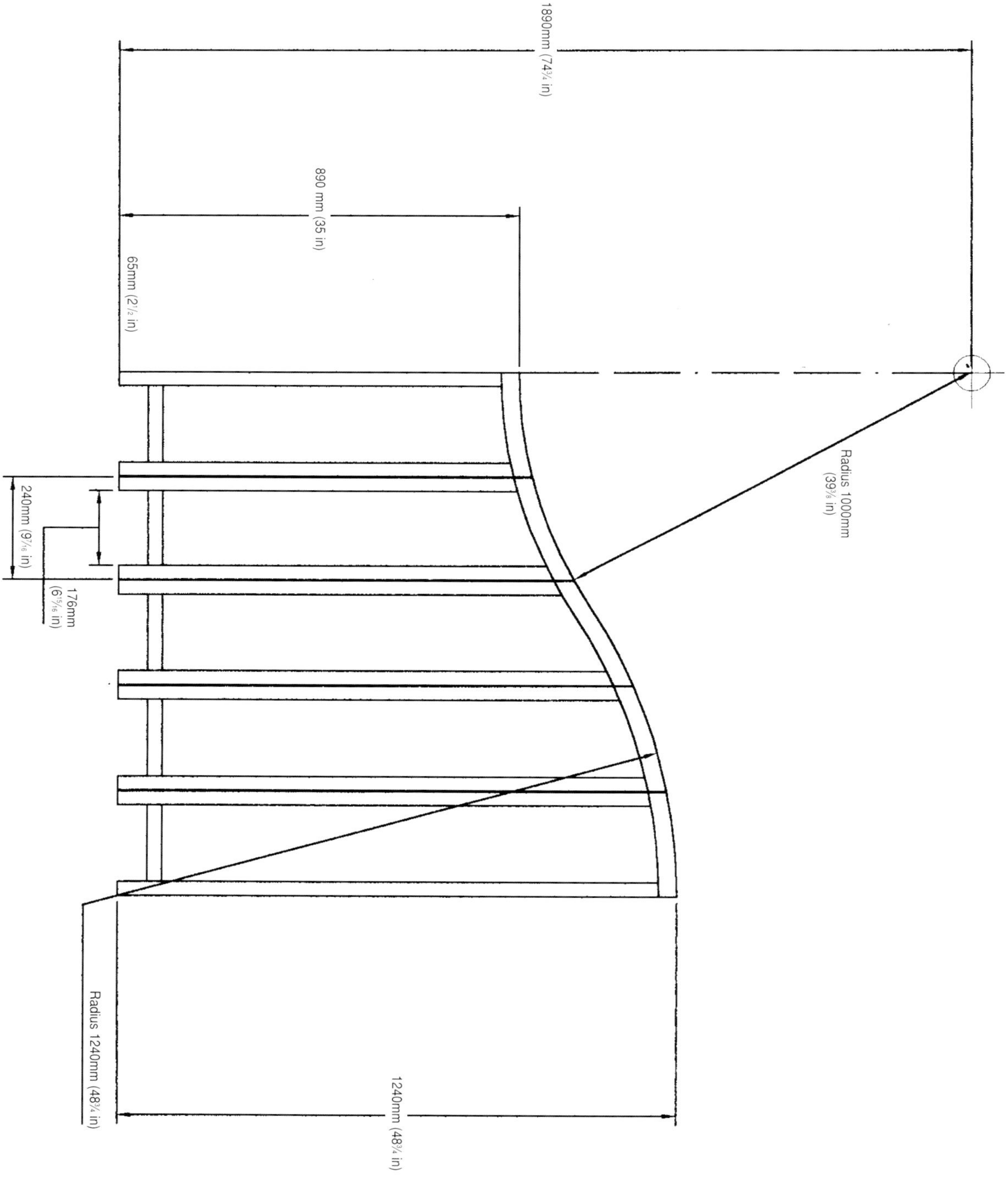

1890mm (74¾ in)
890 mm (35 in)
65mm (2½ in)
Radius 1000mm (39⅜ in)
240mm (9 7/16 in)
176mm (6 15/16 in)
Radius 1240mm (48¾ in)
1240mm (48¾ in)

FIRE SCREEN (SC2)

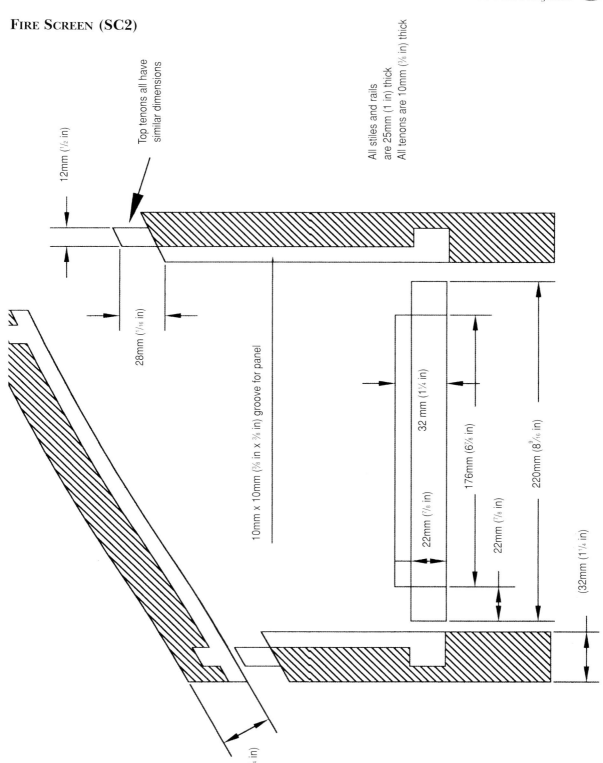

Top tenons all have similar dimensions

12mm ($\frac{1}{2}$ in)

28mm ($\frac{7}{16}$ in)

All stiles and rails are 25mm (1 in) thick
All tenons are 10mm ($\frac{3}{8}$ in) thick

10mm x 10mm ($\frac{3}{8}$ in x $\frac{3}{8}$ in) groove for panel

32 mm (1$\frac{1}{4}$ in)

176mm (6$\frac{7}{8}$ in)

220mm (8$\frac{9}{16}$ in)

22mm ($\frac{7}{8}$ in)

22mm ($\frac{7}{8}$ in)

(32mm (1$\frac{1}{4}$ in))

32mm (1$\frac{1}{4}$ in)

GLOSSARY

Abrade to remove with abrasive material.

Abrasive the scouring action of sandpaper, emery paper or wirewool.

Adhesive glue used for sticking veneers to each other or to a baseboard. Sticky gum used on tape.

Aluminium oxide an abrasive, hardwearing mineral applied to the surface of sandpaper.

Anthemion the honeysuckle ornament much used in plaster work and furniture during the neo-classical period.

Burr or **Burl** the abnormal growth at the base of trees and around the root system. Called Burr in UK and Burl in the USA.

Cross-banding the laying of a veneer such that the grain lays at 90° to its adjacent veneer. Often used to border veneered panels and make decorative bandings.

Cupping timber that distorts in shape, producing a hollowed surface.

Cure the drying time necessary for water-based glues.

Cutting gauge a tool with a sliding fence used to make measured cuts into veneers from the sides of a board.

Fence a guide, either fixed or adjustable, used on machines and handtools to cut straight lines at a pre-set distance.

Fiddleback the rippled maple veneer traditionally used to decorate the backs of violins.

Flute one segment of a marquetry fan.

French polish a generic name given to a polish made from shellac and spirit.

‘G’ Clamp small steel hand clamp for holding woods together. Its profile forms a shape like the letter G, hence its name.

Grain filler a coloured or transparent liquid used to fill the grain of wood, or gaps in fretsaw work, prior to sanding and finishing.

Groundwork a wood board or panel to which decorative veneer and marquetry is glued.

Harewood the mineral process used to create a chemical colour change to certain wood veneers.

Husk the seed pot of corn, used extensively in 18th-century décor on both plasterwork and furniture.

Inlay a thin strip of wood let into a prepared channel.

Jig an appliance for guiding or positioning a tool, to make a task easier to manage.

Lacquer modern cellulose-based finishing material that depends on an additive (catalyst) to kick-start the hardening process.

Laminate bonding together thin layers of wood to form thicker material.

Lipping a thin strip of decorative wood used usually as a contrasting edge or top of other woods.

MDF medium-density fibreboard. A man-made flat board, ideal for veneering work.

Neo-classical a name given to an historic period in furniture and architecture. In Britain the period was about 1770–1800.

Parquetry cutting pieces of wood or veneer into geometric shapes to make a uniform repeating pattern.

Patera a rosette design found in bas-relief in friezes and repeated in marquetry work (plural paterae).

Pigment a powdered substance used to impart colour, used with grain fillers and finishing materials.

PVA (poly-vinyl acetate) a modern water-based transparent adhesive.

Quartered corner A 90° corner broken by an inward-curving quarter-circle radius.

Rebate a recess cut into wood. Also called a rabbit.

Rubber a pad made from cotton wool and wrapped in cotton cloth to apply French polish.

Sandshading a process of scorching wood veneers in hot silver sand to create a dark shadow, for artistic effect in marquetry.

Sanding sealer a methylated spirit or cellulose-based sealant applied prior to finishing polish.

Sandwich a multi-veneered pack, nailed or pinned together prior to fretsawing a pattern.

Sash-clamp A clamp with a long bar used originally for gluing the frames of sash windows.

Scallop the curved ends of flutes used on marquetry fans.

Shellac resin secreted by the lac beetle and dissolved in spirit to make French polish.

Silicon carbide a self-lubricating paper that prevents clogging; mineral substance used to coat fine abrasive finishing paper.

Sliding bevel a tool with a handle and sliding steel arm that can be set to any angle to aid precise cutting and sawing.

Stringing a thin strip of wood used for decoration in furniture and marquetry work.

Swag décor that droops like curtains across a window frame. Used in Robert Adam designs and in 18th-century marquetry.

Template (or templet) a guide used to cut shapes of wood and veneers. Usually used for repeating patterns to ensure uniformity.

Wet or dry an abrasive finishing paper for polishes and paints. Can be used wet or dry.

SUPPLIERS AND REFERENCES

UK SUPPLIERS

Art Veneers
Chiswick Avenue Industrial Estate
Mildenhall
Suffolk
IP28 7AY

website: www.artveneers.co.uk
(veneers, marquetry tools and equipment, marquetry
kits)

John Boddy Timber Ltd
Riverside Sawmills
Boroughbridge
North Yorkshire
YO5 9LJ
email: info@john-boddys-fwts.co.uk
(veneers, marquetry tools and equipment, timber
suppliers)

Shesto Ltd
Unit 2 Sapcote Trading Estate
374 High Street
Willesden
London
NW10 2DH
website: www.shesto.com
(Zona fretsaw blades, gents padsaw, marquetry tools
and equipment)

Optimum Brasses
Castle Street
Bampton, Near Tiverton
Devon
EX16 9NS
website: www.obida.com
(brass gallery tray handles, brass hinges etc.)

The Air Press Company Ltd
Units 5–6, Scott's Close
Downton Business Centre
Downton
Wiltshire
SP5 3RA
website: www.airpress.uk.com
(vacuum presses)

M-Power Tools Ltd
Manor Farm
Newton Tony
Salisbury
Wiltshire
United Kingdom
SP4 0HA
website: www.m-powertools.com
(circle cutter, tri-scribe and tri-blade)

W. H. Smiths
Stationery shops located throughout the country
(bookbinding film)

REFERENCES

Art Veneers Manual and Catalogue, available from
www.artveneers.co.uk

Hawkins, David, *Wood Surface Decoration*, London:
Batsford, 1986

Lincoln, William A., *World Woods in Colour*, London:
Stobart, and New York: Macmillan, 1986

Lincoln, William A., *Marquetry Manual*, London:
Stobart, 1989

Middleton, David, and Alan Townsend, *Marquetry
Techniques*, London: Batsford, 1993

Leeds Marquetry Group: www.leedsmarquetry.org.uk

Harewood House Trust, Harewood, Leeds LS17 9LQ:
www.harewood.org

Temple Newsam House Leeds LS15 0AE:
www.leeds.gov.uk/templenewsam/

Newby Hall and Gardens, Ripon, HG4 5AE:
www.newbyhall.com

INDEX